The Biblical an Observational Case for Geocentricity

A Place rather than a Path for the Earth

IF AT ITS "FASTEST LATITUDE" THE EARTH WITH THE ATMOSPHERE IS SPINNING 1038 MPH AT THE EQUATOR, WHY IS THE EQUATOR CALLED "THE DOLDRUMS"? WHY DOES EARTH'S SUPPOSED SPIN HAVE SO LITTLE EFFECT ON EAST-WEST PLANE FLIGHTS?

Compiled by J. A. Moorman

Foreword

The Author. The author of this present work is Dr. Jack Moorman. He was trained for the ministry in the United States. For many years he served the Lord as a missionary in South Africa. He is now a missionary in the United Kingdom. Dr. Moorman is one of the missionaries supported by The Bible For Today Baptist Church here in Collingswood, New Jersey.

Dr. Moorman's Other Materials. Among the many other materials Dr. Moorman has written and the Bible For Today has published, are the following fourteen titles:

(1) *Biblical Chronology--The Two Great Divides* (**BFT #2934, 158 pages @ $16.00 + S&H**).
(2) The Church–Beginning Baptism Body Bride (**BFT #3337, 40 pages @ $4.00 + S&H**).
(3) The Pretribulation Rapture Defended (**BFT #3347, 33 pages @ $4.00 + S&H**);.
(4) *Psalm 12:6-7 And Bible Preservation* (**BFT #2524, 51 pages @ $4.00 + S&H**).
(5) *1 John 5:7-8 Defended As Genuine--Part Of #1617* (**BFT #2249, 15 pages @ $2.00 + S&H**)
(6) 8000 Differences Between The Critical Text & The TR (**BFT #3084, 543 pages @ $20.00+S&H**)
(7) *Conies, Brass, And Easter--KJB Problems Answered* (**BFT #1737, 38 pages @ $4.00 + S&H**).
(8) *Early Manuscripts And The A.V.--A Closer Look* (**BFT #1825, 157 pages @ $15.00 + S&H**).
(9) *Forever Settled--Bible Documents & History Survey* (**BFT #1428, 217 pages, @ $21.00 + S&H**).
(10) *Missing In Modern Bibles--Nestle-Aland & NIV Errors* (**BFT #1726, 83 pages, @ $8.00 + S&H**).
(11) Manuscript Digest of the N.T. (**BFT #3324, 722 pages @ $361.00 + S&H**).
(12) *Hodges/Farstad 'Majority' Text Refuted By Evidence* (**BFT #1617, 160 pages @ $16.00 + S&H**).
(13) *Doctrinal Heart of the Bible--Removed from Modern Versions* (**BFT #1726VCR @ $15.00 + S&H**).
(14) *Samuel Tregelles & the Critical Text* (**BFT #3195, 12 pages @ $3.00 + S&H**)

The Controversy. Just as in the theory of evolution versus the Biblical teaching and the truth of God's creation, so there is a controversy whether or not both the Bible and scientific facts teach clearly that the earth is the center of God's creation rather than the sun. Dr. Moorman has done a masterful job in clarifying this subject for the Bible-believing Christians.

The Helper. When Dr. Moorman sent his book over to me from England by the email in MS Word format, I had to format it in Word Perfect in order to prepare it properly for printing. Many details had to be straightened out, especially the centering and positioning of the pictures. Dr. Kirk DiVietro, a computer expert, spent many hours helping me with these computer problems. Many thanks!!

My Prayer For The Reader. May the Lord give you an open mind to look into this intricate investigation of both the Bible's statements and those of men of science. It is believed as the author states: From the standpoint of the **Senses**, from the standpoint of **Science**, and most importantly from the standpoint of **Scripture**, there is a strong case to be heard (See pages 9-40).

Yours For God's Words,

D. A. Waite

Pastor D. A. Waite, Th.D., Ph.D.
Bible For Today Baptist Church
900 Park Avenue, Collingswood, New Jersey 08108
Website: BibleForToday.org;
Phone: **856-854-4747**; FAX: **856-854-2464**

Published by

THE BIBLE FOR TODAY PRESS

900 Park Avenue
Collingswood, New Jersey 08108
U.S.A.

Pastor D. A. Waite, Th.D., Ph.D.

𝕭𝖎𝖇𝖑𝖊 𝕱𝖔𝖗 𝕿𝖔𝖉𝖆𝖞 𝕭𝖆𝖕𝖙𝖎𝖘𝖙 𝕮𝖍𝖚𝖗𝖈𝖍

Church Phone: 856-854-4747
BFT Phone: 856-854-4452
Orders: 1-800-John 10:9
e-mail: BFT@BibleForToday.org
Website: www.BibleForToday.org
fax: 856-854-2464

**We Use and Defend
The King James Bible**

**July, 2013
BFT 4054**

ISBN #978-1-56848-086-2

A Word From The Author:

WE DO NOT WANT TO BE FUNDAMENTALLY WRONG CONCERNING THE EARTH ON WHICH GOD HAS PLACED US. WE KNOW THAT DARWINISM IS WRONG. WE KNOW THAT BIG-BANGISM IS WRONG. THIS STUDY PRESENTS THE CASE THAT COPERNICANISM IS ALSO WRONG, AND IN FACT PAVED THE WAY FOR DARWINISM. AS WITH DARWINISM, COPERNICANISM BECAME ESTABLISHED WITHOUT EMPIRICAL EVIDENCE. A SUBSTANTIAL CASE CAN BE MADE FOR THE GEOCENTRIC VIEW; BUT AS THIS IS A MATTER BARELY CONSIDERED TODAY, IT IS BEST TO SAY THAT THE VIEWS EXPRESSED ARE THOSE OF THE AUTHOR AND NOT NECESSARILY OF BETHEL BAPTIST CHURCH, LONDON OR OTHER GROUPS WITH WHICH THE AUTHOR FELLOWSHIPS.

Table of Contents
(Updated–June, 2013)

Why Does the Atmosphere *Not* Move Strongly to the West?
Why *Do* Jet Streams Move to the East?
How Can the Equatorial "Doldrums" Be Spinning At 1038 mph?
Why Do Westward Flights *Not* Arrive Sooner?

The Biblical and Observational Case for Geocentricity

A Place Rather than a Path for the Earth

Introduction

Before we leave this world we want to be certain that we have *not* made a fundamental error concerning the creation in which God has placed us (See Psalms 28:5). This is especially so if it is a matter to which both the Bible and common sense seem clearly to support.

Among believers in the full inspiration and preservation of Holy Scripture there has been a renewed interest in what for most would be termed "the unthinkable." The view is known as *geocentricity*, in which the earth is at rest, and the sun, moon and stars travel around the earth. Or, as in the words of a leading spokesman:

> We maintain that the Bible teaches us of an earth that neither rotates daily nor revolves yearly about the sun; that it is at rest with respect to the throne of Him who called it into existence and that hence it is absolutely at rest in the universe (Gerardus D. Bouw, *The Biblical Astronomer*, Credo).

This was the cosmology for some 5,700 years of man's 6000-year tenure on earth. This is what the senses assumed. This is what everyone believed. In fact history records *only two* heliocentric astronomers before Copernicus: A Greek, Aristarchus of Samos (d. 230 BC), and Seleucus of Seleucia, a Mesopotamian astronomer who lived around 150BC. More importantly, this is what *everyone* believed the Bible to teach. The Bible was always assumed to be a Geocentric Book.

Very few today are aware of the extent of the issue that presented itself to Bible believers three hundred years ago. There was no precedent for a perceived teaching of Scripture to have been held for so long, so continuously, so universally, and then to be so completely replaced by another. Nor was there precedent for the Bible to be contradicted by a later discovery. This was not another debate over the interpretation of Scripture; the acceptance of a spinning and orbiting earth was viewed as an attack upon the authority of Scripture itself.

If history has consistently used the word *Revolution* to describe an event, there is every likelihood that this is in fact what it was - an event of epic proportion! And more so if there is not any geographic (French, Russian) or other limitation given to the event. The fire Copernicus lit was called a "Revolution." It was a revolution in the fullest sense of the word. It completely reshaped the way men thought about the world and of life itself. Only something on this scale could have prepared the way for Darwinism. And, note that even that was not called a "revolution."

Simply put, Bible believers up to the time of Copernicus understood that the Scriptures not only tell how we go to heaven, but also *how the heavens go.*

There are many *down to earth* considerations that are seldom thought about today.

1.   The Bible, and notably the King James Bible, is a *Geocentric Book.* A substantial number of passages beginning with Genesis One show a *fixed earth* to be assumed. There is nothing in Scripture that points to a rotating, orbiting earth. The argument claiming passages depicting a stationary earth give only the "language of appearance" soon begins to run thin. It is always: *He appointed the moon for seasons: the sun knoweth his going down* (Psalm 104:19). This is an impossible concept to reconcile with heliocentricity! How could the sun know *its going down* if it is not going down, and if instead the earth is turning beneath the sun? To speak of this as poetic language ignores the fact that the first half of the verse is clearly not poetic. Both the sun and the moon exactly observe the *appointments* of their Creator.

2.   In reading Genesis One, most skip over a number of key implications concerning the First, Second and Fourth Days of the Creation Week. Inadequate attention is given; to the *non-mention* of any earth motion; to the question "what was the earth orbiting before the Fourth Day"; to the fact that the firmament created on the Second Day is in fact called *the firmament*; that it is a great deal more than "an expanse" as translated by the modern versions; that it is completely separate and distinct from the earth created on the First Day (see also Exodus 20:11; 31:17), and that it is able to receive the sun, moon and stars which were created and *set in* the firmament on the Fourth Day. These factors clearly point to a central and stationary earth.

3.   The system of Tycho Brahe (died 1601) in which the planets as well as the stars are centered upon the sun, and all of which, in turn, orbits a stationary earth, is shown to be in harmony with observational data. The vast number and accuracy of planetary and star calculations amassed by Tycho Brahe (likely history's greatest astronomer!) are shown to this day to be remarkably accurate. They demonstrate with slight revision that the geocentric position is completely workable.

4.   The researches of Copernicus, Kepler, Galileo and Newton *did not* produce clear proof that the earth both rotates on an axis and orbits the sun. Yet this view became firmly established in the world's universities by the mid-17th Century. The rush to acceptance *without empirical proof* would be repeated in the stampede toward Darwinism.

5.   The primary impetus for Einstein's 1905 *Theory of Special Relativity* was the so-called "unsatisfactory" results of the Michelson and Morley light experiments of the 1880s. In this oft-repeated experiment two simultaneous light beams are sent out and back along two arms of an interferometer. One is in the direction of the earth's assumed orbit around the sun, the other over the same distance at right angles. The right-angle beam should return slightly sooner. This is because the amount of time the other beam spends moving with the velocity of the earth (66,780 mph) and through the medium of space (called the ether) is not enough to compensate for the time it spends moving against this velocity. Though repeated with ever greater precision unto the present day, the results are the same; the light beams return at about the same time, showing virtually no movement of the earth.

This caused great consternation in the scientific community. Fitzgerald proposed "conveniently" that the earth's speed caused the arm aimed in the orbital direction to *shrink* slightly, thus enabling the beam to return at the same time. Einstein brought this *shrinking* concept into his bizarre 1905 theory in which objects are supposed to become more "narrow" as they approach the speed of light. Einstein further denied the existence of the ether as a medium.

In fact by this kind of reasoning *everything on earth must be wider than they actually appear*, for if the supposed velocity of the earth's rotation is added to its velocity around the sun, and then adding the velocity of the solar system through the galaxy, and finally the speed of the galaxy through space, we would be travelling at nearly two million mph!

6.   It is said that for "convenience but not *in reality*" the satellite system, and the space program generally, is based on *fixed earth coordinates*. As one example, the Geostationary Satellite "parked" at an extremely high altitude appears to be stationary over a fixed point on the Equator. There are two possible explanations as to how this works. Which is the more plausible ?

        (1) At an altitude of 22,236 miles the satellite is kept aloft by its *orbital velocity* of 6,856 mph, and over a daily circumference of 164,560 miles, maintains an exact position over a spot on the earth spinning at 1038 mph.

        (2) At an altitude of 22,236 miles the satellite is kept aloft by *equilibrium* between earth's gravity and the pull of a *spinning* universe, and the *stationary* satellite maintains an exact position over a spot on the *stationary* earth.

    Given, that in order for the world's TVs and a host of other applications to work at all, there must be perfect synchronization of these vast velocities and distances; the fixed earth explanation is far more plausible. Further, the proposed *elevator* satellite gives an insight into the true nature of fixed earth coordinates. *They show that the earth is fixed.*

7.   "Some may question if the geocentric model would make it impossible for NASA to predict spacecraft orbits etc. This is easily dealt with.

Assume you are looking at an orrery - a mechanical machine with the planets on long arms rotating around the sun which is at the centre. In this machine the sun is stationary at the centre

and the planets rotate around it and also spin on their axis. This is the accepted way in which the planets move around the sun.

    Now imagine that, while it is working, you pick the whole machine up by holding the earth. Everything now rotates about the earth, but their relative positions as they go round the sun and to each other are exactly the same as before. Einstein's relativity does not come into it.

    "What people do not realise is that NASA works out every spacecraft trajectory related to the earth - as though the earth were the centre of the planetary system. This is NOT presented as further scientific evidence as it is only used to make the maths easier, but it is interesting nevertheless." (Malcolm Bowden).

8.   It is claimed that the earth's *easterly* rotation is a major factor in wind and atmospheric patterns (known as the Coriolis Effect). However if this were the case the easterly rotation should also cause a prevailing

westerly drift of the atmosphere. It must be both or neither. In reality, not only do we see generally prevailing *easterly* weather systems, but also jet streams in *both* the northern and southern hemisphere, moving *easterly* and much faster than the supposed rotation of the earth. Further, with the earth "spinning 1038 mph on the Equator" we should see *daily hurricanes*! With *angular momentum*, extreme weather would be the only result as winds move north and south from the rapidly moving Equator to "slower" latitudes. Instead we have the opposite – *doldrums* on the equator!

There is much more! The weather we experience is simply not going to be possible if the 300 mile high atmosphere is *riding upon* a spinning and orbiting earth. This simple fact *well explains* why the climate scientists and long distance airline pilots *play down* the effects caused by earth's rotation.

9.   It is obvious that an object or person can only share fully in the velocity of the earth's rotation *if it is directly attached to the earth*. Once there is a "disconnect" and the object is suspended above the earth, the inertia, velocity and momentum received from the "spinnearth *can only decrease*. Gravity and the atmosphere may slow the rate of decrease, but this decrease must soon become apparent, and this especially so in east – west flying. With the earth said to be spinning from west to east, cities *would move toward* west bound flights, thus greatly shortening the flight time. With east bound planes it will be "a very long flight" as it seeks to *catch up* with its eastward moving destination.

That there can be *no other* result for east-west and west-east flights on a spinning earth is *so obvious*, and is *so ignored* today, I think you will be *so amazed* when you see how this is "explained" by long distance pilots.

 10.   There are many anomalies with heliocentricity, for example, it is said that the rotation of the earth has caused an *equatorial bulge* with earth's radius to the equator to be 13.25 miles greater than the radius to the poles. What effect would this *equatorial bulge* have on a long south flowing river like the Mississippi?

> "New Orleans, which is located at about 29 degrees north latitude, happens to be nearly three miles farther from the earth's center than Lake Itasca, Minn., headwaters of the Mississippi River, which is situated a shade under 47 degrees north latitude. Thus, Old Man River is forced to flow uphill on its 2,340-mile journey to the Gulf of Mexico."
> (http://www.travelersjournal.com/articles2.php?ID=291).

In short: *How can we (and the atmosphere!) be hurtling along in a multi-directional velocity of Two Million MPH and be totally oblivious of it?*

From the standpoint of the *Senses*, from the standpoint of *Science*, and most importantly from the standpoint of *Scripture*, there is a *strong case* to be heard.

Jack Moorman
London
June 2013

Part I: What the Senses Observe

Nightly the magnificent display of interconnected groups of stars known as constellations rotate overhead. The entire sky, north and south, is divided into 88 of these constellations. For example in the constellation *Ursa Minor*, Polaris, the North Star, is seen at the end of the handle of the Little Dipper. The 12 constellations in the band along the path of the Sun (with the Moon and planets) form the Zodiac. During the year the Sun appears to travel backwards through these 12 constellations. While we see both the Sun and stars rotating daily from east to west, the sun is seen to be moving slightly slower, thus its backward motion. The mean solar day is exactly 24 hours; but the "star" or sidereal day (*sidus* is Latin for star) is 23 hours, 56 minutes, 4.1 seconds. This allows for one additional sidereal day for every 365 solar days.

A geocentric cosmology is what people saw and what their senses took for granted. Daily and nightly the stars along with the Sun, Moon and planets were seen rotating from east to west overhead. It never occurred to them that it was the earth's surface that was spinning from west to east beneath these heavenly bodies. They did not "adjust to the fact" that the stars and the Sun were fixed. And, that though the Moon was moving, it was actually moving in the opposite direction and much slower than what they observed. Their cosmology was simply a common knowledge based on *sight* and *sense*.

The North Star and circumpolar stars in a photograph with a long shutter speed of several hours. Note that the stars near the celestial pole make less of a trail with the long exposure. ("Circumpolar Star" *Wikipedia*).

From a vantage point in the northern hemisphere they would watch the stars rotate around Polaris - the Polar or North Star. It was their unquestioned belief that the stars were spinning overhead. The star trails from time-lapse photography give the same impression. Polaris lines up vertically with earth's North Pole and forms the North Pole (or nearly so) of what was long known as the Celestial Sphere - the large hemispherical dome onto which the celestial bodies appear to be affixed. Polaris is never seen to change its position in the sky - regardless of the time of year. If our latitude is 50 degrees (a little below London), we will see Polaris due north above earth's North Pole, and at an angle of about 50 degrees from our vantage point.

All stars in the northern hemisphere, whether in a wide or small radius, are seen circling Polaris, and are known as Circumpolar Stars. This term is given to a star that, due to its proximity to one of the celestial poles as viewed from a given latitude, never sets (i.e. it never disappears below the horizon). Circumpolar stars are therefore visible from the same location towards nearest pole for the entire night on every night of the year (and would be continuously visible throughout the day also, were they not overwhelmed by the Sun's glare).

It is interesting to note that the original meaning of "Arctic Circle" meant "Circle of the Bears" (Ursa Major, the Great Bear; and Ursa Minor, the Little Bear), from the Greek *arktikos*, "near the Bear." ("Circumpolar Star" *Wikipedia*).

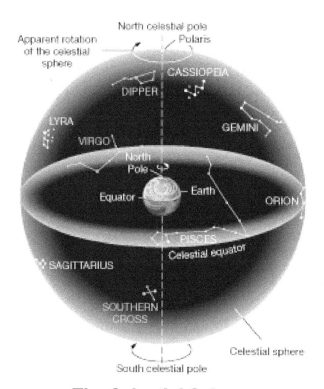

The Celestial Sphere

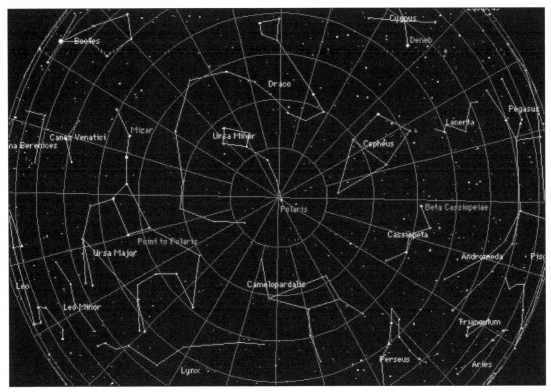

The Northern Constellations

The Zodiac Constellations

Except during periods of light, daily (24 hours minus 4 minutes) we see the stars complete one 360° rotation around the Polar Star axis. The four-minute difference enables the constellations to rotate a little further each day from east to west in relation to the Sun and for part of the year cannot be seen because of the Sun. The 4 minute-difference with the sun's "backward" motion among the constellations account for the different sky views we have during the year. When the Sun is "in" a constellation, the constellation will not be seen.

Of this nightly display the Scriptures declare:

> *The heavens declare the glory of God; and the firmament sheweth his handiwork. Day unto day uttereth speech, and night unto night sheweth knowledge. There is no speech nor language, where their voice is not heard.* (Psalms 19:1-3)

Satan has perverted this *voice* in the paganism of Astrology. For an explanation of how the constellations of the Zodiac may well picture Christ and the Gospel, see *The Witness of the Stars* by E. W. Bullinger, and *The Gospel in the Stars* by Joseph Seiss. See also below on Job 38:31-33. For an excellent view of the constellations circling daily around Polaris see: http://stellarium.org/

Part II: What the Bible Declares

A Perceived Violation of Scripture

More important than *sight* and *sense*, is *Scripture*. Geocentricity was the belief system accepted by virtually all who held to the Scriptures - Jewish, Christian, Protestant, Catholic, learned, unlearned. It was believed because men assumed it to be the teaching of the Bible. Indeed, if one will give a careful reading to *Day One*, *Day Two*, and *Day Four* in Genesis One, and then go on to the considerable number of further passages in the Bible, a geocentric conclusion is quite natural. In fact, it is compelling!

When one considers these passages, it is difficult to believe that Bible readers over those long centuries were but reading *the language of appearance* or were being "accommodated for" because of their pre scientific viewpoint. We do not see the Bible making this kind of adaptation with regard to other subjects. These Scriptures were believed to be a revelation. They went beyond what man could naturally see and know. If the Bible were but a retelling of what men saw, then of course it ceases to be a revelation. There is nothing revelatory about the language of appearance! Thus when this ancient belief system was overthrown through the influence of Copernicus (1473-1543), Kepler (1571-1630), and Galileo (1564-1642), there was the sense that the Bible had been directly violated.

Every student is taught how the medieval Catholic Church opposed Galileo and was able for a time to silence both his views and ban the *De Revolutionibus Orbium Coelestium* of Copernicus. However, it should be pointed out that minds much more sound in faith than that of Papal Rome were greatly exercised as to what was happening. An example of the Reformation view at the time can be seen from the following well-known commentators:

> The heavens revolve daily; immense as is their fabric, and inconceivable the rapidity of their revolutions, (John Calvin on Psa. 93:1).

> ...*day and night, summer and winter,* which are interchanged by the motion of the sun, (Matthew Henry, Gen. 1:14-19).

> *Let there be lights*...1. By their motions and influences to produce and distinguish the four seasons...2. By their diurnal and swift motion to make the days, (Matthew Poole, Gen. 1:14).

John Owen and John Wesley were clear in their opposition to Copernicus.

> Dr. John Owen, so famous in the annals of Puritanism, declared the Copernican system a "delusive and arbitrary hypothesis, contrary to Scripture"; and even John Wesley declared the new ideas to "tend toward infidelity". (Andrew White, *A History of the Warfare of Science with Theology in Christendom*, p.123).

As late as the nineteenth century the respected commentator John Gill allowed for both options on the first three days of creation, that is, that either the light source created on the first day moved around the earth, or the earth rotated. Only with the creation of the sun on day four did he insist on the earth's rotation.

Luther, Melanchthon and other reformers spoke against the new view because they believed the authority of Scripture was at stake. It certainly was not an "ill informed, pre-scientific tirade", when Luther in referring to Copernicus said:

> A certain new astrologer who wanted to prove that the earth moves and not the sky, the sun and the moon…I believe the Holy Scriptures, for Joshua commanded the sun to stand still and not the earth, (*Table Talks*; vol. 54; pp. 358,359).

Writing six years after Copernicus death, Luther's associate, Melanchthon, wrote:

> The eyes are witnesses that the heavens revolve in the space of twenty-four hours. But certain men, either from the love of novelty, or to make a display of ingenuity, have concluded that the earth moves; and they maintain that neither the eighth sphere nor the sun revolves…Now, it is a want of honesty and decency to assert such notions publicly, and the example is pernicious. It is the part of a good mind to accept the truth as revealed by God and to acquiesce in it. (Thomas S. Kuhn, The Copernican Revolution, p. 191.)

In his commentary on Genesis, Calvin cited Psalm 93:1: *The earth also is established, that it cannot be moved*. He then went on to say:

> Who will venture to place the authority of Copernicus above that of the Holy Spirit? (Kuhn p. 192).

Believers in that previous time did indeed believe that "the earth was at rest with respect to the throne of Him who had called it into being." The earth neither revolved nor rotated, all movement in the universe was with respect to the earth. This is what they understood the Bible to say and mean. *The heaven is my throne, and the earth is my footstool*, Isa. 66:1. Far from swinging by orbital gravity from the sun, the earth was hung by God *upon nothing*, Job 26:7. It was *founded* and *laid as a foundation*, Prov. 3:19; Heb. 1:10. It was *stable*, I Chron. 16:30. It was *set upon pillars*, I Sam. 2:8. It *could not be moved*, Psa. 93:1. If it did *move out of its place*, it was because of judgement, Isa. 13:13. Rather than the earth moving, it is *the stars in their courses*, and the *sun going forth in his might*, Job 5:20,31. It is the sun that *knows its going down*, Psa. 104:19; and that *stood still in its habitation*, Hab. 3:11. In the future Tribulation Period *the sun will go down at noon*, Amos 8:9. If *the Sun of Righteousness arises*, so in like manner *the sun also rises*, Mal. 1:11; 4:2. If the winds and rivers are in constant motion, so the sun is also in motion, *and ariseth, goeth down, hasteth to its place*, yet *the earth abideth*, Eccl. 1:4-7.

Early Heliocentricists Knew They Were Violating Scripture

Copernicus, Kepler and Galileo where aware that their heliocentricity was at variance with the Bible.

Copernicus when responding to Luther's charge, and his evoking Joshua 10:13 said:
> To attack me by twisting a passage from Scripture is the resort of one who claims

judgement upon things he does not understand.   Mathematics is written only for mathematicians. (R. Thiel, *And There Was Light*, p. 88).

Copernicus is in effect saying that mathematics supersedes the Bible.

We will show later that mathematics became something of an "art form" in its adaptation to heliocentricity.

Johannes Kepler (1571-1630) trained for the Lutheran priesthood, but was not ordained because of unorthodox views. Regarding astronomy, he believed the Scriptures "employed popular speech in order to be understood".

> ...astronomy discloses the causes of natural phenomena and takes within its purview the investigation of optical illusions. Much loftier subjects are treated by Holy Writ, which employs popular speech in order to be understood. With in this framework and with a different purpose in view, only in passing does the Scripture touch on the appearances of natural phenomena as they are presented to sight, ... the sun stands still, turns back, rises, sets, goes forth from one end of heaven like a bridegroom coming out of his chamber....These expressions are used by us...even though not one of these locutions is literally true.... (*Epitomie Astronomiae Copernicanae*, end of Book I).

Galileo in a letter dated 21 December 1613 wrote:

> It was moreover necessary in Scripture. In order that it be accommodated to the general understanding, to say things quite diverse... from absolute truth ... Hence it appears that physical effects placed before our eyes by sensible experience, or concluded by necessary demonstration, should not in any circumstances be called in doubt by passages in Scripture...(S. Drake, *Galileo at Work--His Scientific Biography*, p. 225)

And again in 1613:

> In questions concerning the natural sciences Holy Writ must occupy the last place...(Dominique Tassot, "Galileo and Modern Exegesis," *Bulletin of the Tychonian Society*, Spring 1990, p. 4).

However, in a 29 March 1641 letter in which he deems as "fallacious and erroneous" the Ptolemaic system, Galileo very surprisingly had some other things to say:

> The falsity of the Copernican system must not on any account be doubted, especially by us Catholics, who have the irrefragable authority of the Holy Scriptures interpreted by the greatest masters in theology, whose agreement renders us certain of the stability of the earth and the mobility of the sun around it. (Drake, pp. 417,418).

In contrast, Tycho Brahe (d. 1601) whose astronomical observations far exceeded those of Copernicus, Kepler and Galileo, knew that this was an issue that involved the integrity of the Scriptures.

Tycho prized parts of the Copernican doctrine or at least acknowledged the abilities of its originator, but could not bring himself to accept a sun–centered universe. His reluctance to do so can be ascribed partly to his respect for Scripture and partly to his feeling of common sense, but largely to his inability to conceive of a universe so immense that an observer as accurate as he knew himself to be could not detect any stellar parallax, the necessary consequence of the earth's motion around the sun (http://www.encyclopedia.com/topic/Tycho_Brahe.aspx).

What was the basis of Tycho's rejection of the Copernican system? Let Tycho tell us in his own (translated) words.

Since all these results [parallax measurements of Mars and Venus] did not all agree with the Ptolemaic hypotheses I was urged afterward to put more and more confidence in the Copernican invention. The exceedingly absurd opinion that the Earth revolves uniformly and perpetually nevertheless made up a very great obstacle, and in addition the irrefutable authority of the Holy Scripture maintained the opposite view (http://astroblogger.blogspot.co.uk/2009/04/tycho-brahe-gets-shave.html).

Geocentric Passages Become the "Language of Appearance"

With the advent of heliocentrism, it became apparent that a fundamental shift had taken place. Scripture was at this point surrendered. The Bible still told us how we go to heaven, but the Bible gives no factual revelation as to *how the heavens go* - how they go in reference to the earth.

What had long been thought to be statements of fact now became statements of appearance and hyperbole (a deliberate exaggeration used for effect). Passages like Isaiah 55:12 began to be given as examples of how geocentric passages were to be read, *For ye shall go out with joy, and be led forth with peace: the mountains and the hills shall break forth before you into singing, and all the trees of the field shall clap their* hands. Unless one wants to use this kind of passage as a pretext to symbolize the Bible's literal statements (as amillennialists do with the prophetic Scriptures), the application of these passages is clear and obvious to the Bible believer. It is an expression of heightened human emotion. We would not dream of using this as a precedent for interpreting geocentric passages. Trees never clap their hands, hills never sing, but passages concerning the movement of the sun, moon and stars with reference to the earth can by contrast be naturally construed as literal statements of fact.

The Bible's literal geocentric passages were surrendered to hyperbole and then for the most part ignored all together.

Earth and Heaven Become the "Universe"

A fundamental shift was also perceived in the Biblical distinction between heaven (the second heavens) and earth. Genesis One describes the creation of the earth on the first day, the firmament on the second day, and the sun, moon and stars on the fourth day. Each is presented as a separate entity. On the fourth day the sun, moon and stars were set in the firmament of heaven. Hence in the Biblical cosmology, the earth is clearly distinct from both the firmament of heaven and the bodies placed in the firmament.

Heliocentricity removes this distinction, and makes the earth merely another celestial body in the universe.

Thomas Strouse writes:

> The *Good New s Bible* incorrectly translates Genesis 1:1 as "In the beginning when God created the universe.".… The Latin-derived word "universe" comes from universum and literally means "turned into one." For the Christian the Bible consistently gives the biblical term "heaven and earth," the expression for the "worlds" God created (Hebrews 11:3). The Bible neither speaks of the "universe" nor the "solar system," nor calls earth a "planet." (*He Maketh His Sun to Rise: A Biblical Look at Geocentricity*, p. 18).

A secular source says:

> The sharp distinction between heaven and earth was basic in the view of the universe that was accepted by Copernicus' contemporaries. Copernicus comprehended the true nature of the earth. He fully understood that it is a planet revolving about the sun, in the company of other planets. Therefore, like its fellow planets, it too is a heavenly body. Since the earth itself is in the heavens, the contrast between heaven and earth vanished, being replaced by the modern concept of space, (*Encyclopaedia Americana*).

The earth was no longer in the center and at rest with reference to God on His Throne. The earth was now merely another planet: a word that means "wanderer". The Scriptures had been surrendered to Copernicus and Galileo. Scripture would increasingly be subjugated to the theories of science. The acceptance of heliocentricism soon led to acentricism: no centre in the universe. The way was now cleared to take on board the rationalism that was to sweep Europe, and not long after the ultimate surrender: *Darwinism*.

Again we repeat: There is no precedent for a perceived teaching of Scripture having been held for so long, so continuously, so universally, and then to be so completely replaced by another. Nor is there precedent for the Bible to be contradicted by later discoveries shown and proven to be true. The Bible is never contradicted by reality!

John Gill: Halting Between Two Opinions

John Gill (died 1771) the famed Bible commentator and a predecessor to Charles Spurgeon in what became the Metropolitan Tabernacle, was in two minds on this question. Though saying that the earth turned on its axis on Day Four, he allowed that it could either be the light or the earth that was in motion on the first three days.

Regarding the light of the First Day, Gill said:

> But others more rightly take it to be different from the sun, and a more glimmering light, which afterwards was gathered into and perfected in the body of the sun. It is the opinion of Zanchius, and which is approved of by our countryman, Mr. Fuller, that it was a lucid body, or a small lucid cloud, which by its circular motion from east to west made day and night; perhaps somewhat like the cloudy pillar of fire that guided the Israelites in the wilderness, and had no doubt heat as well as light, (*Exposition of the Old Testament*).

In his comments on Genesis 1:5, Gill allowed for both views:

> *And God called the light day, and the darkness he called night...* Either by the circulating motion of the above body of light, or by the rotation of the chaos on its own axis towards it, in the space of twenty four hours there was a vicissitude of light and darkness; just as there is now by the like motion either of the sun, or of the earth; and which after this appellation God has given, we call the one, day, and the other, night.

He then restates the following for the first three days:

> To divide the day from the night; which is the peculiar use of the sun, which by its appearance and continuance makes the day, and by withdrawing itself, or not appearing for a certain time, makes the night; <u>as the light by its circular motion did for the first three days, or the diurnal motion of the earth on its axis, then and now</u>. (Emphasis mine).

But at Day Four, with no reason, grammatical or otherwise, Gill gives only the earth's rotation as the means for the alternating day and night.

The Foundation of the Earth: 21 Passages

The term *foundation* is used for the creation of the earth. This is in contrast to the heavens that are *stretched out*, and strongly implies a geocentric and non-moving earth.

- *for the <u>pillars</u> of the earth are the LORD'S, and he hath set the world upon them.* I Samuel 2:8.
- *Where wast thou when I laid the <u>foundations</u> of the earth? declare, if thou hast understanding.* Job 38:4.
- *Whereupon are the <u>foundations</u> thereof fastened? or who laid the <u>corner stone</u> thereof.* Job 38:6.
- *Of old hast thou laid the <u>foundation</u> of the earth: and the heavens are the work of thy hands.* Psalm 102:25.
- *Who laid the <u>foundations</u> of the earth, that it should not be removed for ever.* Psalm 104:5.
- *The LORD by wisdom hath <u>founded</u> the earth; by understanding hath he established the heavens.* Proverbs 3:19.
- *Have ye not known? have ye not heard? hath it not been told you from the beginning? have ye not understood from the <u>foundations</u> of the earth?* Isaiah 40:21.
- *Mine hand also hath laid the <u>foundation</u> of the earth, and my right hand hath <u>spanned</u> the heavens.* Isaiah 48:13.
- *And forgettest the LORD thy maker, that hath <u>stretched forth</u> the heavens, and laid the <u>foundations</u> of the earth.* Isaiah 51:13.
- *the LORD, which <u>stretcheth forth</u> the heavens, and <u>layeth the foundation</u> of the earth.* Zechariah 12:1.
- *I will utter things which have been kept secret from the <u>foundation</u> of the world.* Matthew 13:35.
- *inherit the kingdom prepared for you from the <u>foundation</u> of the world.* Matthew 25:34.
- *That the blood of all the prophets, which was shed from the <u>foundation</u> of the world.* Luke

11:50.

- *for thou lovedst me before the <u>foundation</u> of the world.* John 17:24.
- *According as he hath chosen us in him before the <u>foundation</u> of the world.* Ephesians 1:4.
- *And, Thou, Lord, in the beginning hast laid the <u>foundation</u> of the earth; and the heavens are the works of thine hands.* Hebrews 1:10.
- *although the works were finished from the <u>foundation</u> of the world.* Hebrews 4:3.
- *For then must he often have suffered since the <u>foundation</u> of the world.* Hebrews 9:26.
- *Who verily was foreordained before the <u>foundation</u> of the world.* I Peter 1:20.
- *whose names are not written in the book of life of the Lamb slain from the <u>foundation</u> of the world.* Revelation 13:8.
- *whose names were not written in the book of life from the <u>foundation</u> of the world.* Revelation 17:8.

Note again: Scripture never speaks about the foundation of the sun, moon and stars.

The Non-movement of the Earth
(Except During End Time Judgements): 12 Passages

Except during times of judgement there is no passage of Scripture which speaks of the Earth moving. It declares the contrary that *it cannot be moved.*

- *Fear before him, all the earth: the world also shall be <u>stable, that it be not moved</u>.* I Chronicles 16:30.
- *Which shaketh the earth out of <u>her place</u>, and the pillars thereof tremble.* Job 9:6.
- *Let all the earth fear the LORD: let all the inhabitants of the world stand in awe of him. For he spake, and it was done; he commanded, and <u>it stood fast</u>.* Psalm 33:8,9.
- *And he built his sanctuary like high palaces, like the earth which he hath <u>established</u> for ever.* Psalm 78.69.
- *the world also is <u>stablished, that it cannot be moved</u>. Thy throne is <u>established</u> of old.* Psalm 93:1,2.
- *The LORD reigneth; let the people tremble: he sitteth between the cherubims; let the earth <u>be moved</u>.* Psalm 99:1.
- *Who laid the foundations of the earth, that it should <u>not be removed</u> for ever.* Psalm 104:5.
- *thou hast <u>established</u> the earth, and it <u>abideth</u>.* Psalm 119:90.
- the earth shall remove out of <u>her place</u>. Isaiah 13:13.
- the earth is <u>moved exceedingly</u>. Isaiah 24:19.
- The heaven is my throne, and the earth is <u>my footstool</u>. Isaiah 61:1.
- Heaven is my throne, and earth is <u>my footstool</u>. Acts 7:49.

The Stretching Out of the Heavens: 12 Passages

The heavenly firmament was stretched and spread out on the Second Day. The Sun, Moon and Stars were set within the firmament on the Fourth Day. The *founding* of the earth and the *stretching out* of the heavenly firmament are frequently distinguished in the Scriptures and point clearly to a geocentric conclusion.

- *Which alone spreadeth out the heavens.* Job 9:8
- *He stretcheth out the north over the empty place.* Job 26:7.
- *Hast thou with him spread out the sky.* Job 37:18
- *Who coverest thyself with light as with a garment: who stretchest out the heavens like a curtain.* Psalm 104:2.
- *It is he that sitteth upon the circle of the earth, and the inhabitants thereof are as grasshoppers; that stretcheth out the heavens as a curtain, and spreadeth them out as a tent to dwell in.* Isaiah 40:22.
- *Thus saith God the LORD, he that created the heavens, and stretched them out.* Isaiah 42:5.
- *Thus saith the LORD…that stretcheth forth the heavens alone.* Isaiah 44:24.
- *I, even my hands, have stretched out the heavens, and all their host have I commanded.* Isaiah 45:12.
- *my right hand hath spanned the heavens.* Isaiah 48:13.
- *And forgettest the LORD thy maker, that hath stretched forth the heavens.* Isaiah 51:13.
- *and hath stretched out the heavens by his discretion.* Jeremiah 10:12.
- *and hath stretched out the heaven by his understanding.* Jeremiah 51:15.

The Movement of the Sun: 58 Passages

"Everyone knows" the earth rotates beneath, and revolves around the sun! This, though, is not what our senses perceive, and Scripture in *every instance* states the opposite. To say that the following passages merely give the "language of appearance" ignores what clearly took place on the First, Second and Fourth Days of the Creation Week. It ignores that Genesis One presents the sun in a secondary sense to the earth. It further ignores the number of passages where action is exercised upon the sun.

- *Sun, stand thou still upon Gibeon. Joshua 10:12*
- *and the sun stood still. Joshua 10:13*
- *Which commandeth the sun and it riseth not. Job 9:7*
- *Which is as a bridegroom coming out of his chamber. Psalm 19:5*
- *His going forth…his circuit. Psalm 19:6*
- *the sun knoweth his going down. Psalm 104:19*
- *The sun also ariseth, and the sun goeth down and hasteth to the place where he arose. Ecclesiastes 1:5*
- *the sun shall be darkened in his going forth. Isaiah 13:10*
- *so the sun returned ten degrees. Isaiah 38:8*
- *I will cause the sun to go down at noon. Amos 8:9*
- *the sun and moon stood still in their habitation. Habakkuk 3:11*

These statements showing action exerted upon the sun set a clear precedent for the following passages, and indicate that the motion stated is actual. Note, that frequently in the context of these statements *someone* or *something* is also said to be moving. Again, how can one be actual and the other figurative?

- *And when the sun was going down. Genesis 15:12*
- *when the sun went down. Genesis 15:17*
- *The sun was risen upon the earth. Genesis 19:23.*

- *because the sun was set.* Genesis 28:11.
- *the sun rose.* Genesis 32:31
- *until the going down of the sun.* Exodus 17:12
- *if the sun be risen upon him.* Exodus 22:3
- *the sun goeth down.* Exodus 22:26
- *And when the sun is down.* Leviticus 22:7
- *toward the rising of the sun.* Numbers 2:3
- *the way where the sun goeth down.* Deuteronomy 11:30
- *at the going down of the sun.* Deuteronomy 16:6
- *when the sun is down.* Deuteronomy 23:11
- *when the sun goeth down.* Deuteronomy 24:13
- *neither shall the sun go down upon it.* Deuteronomy 24:15
- *the going down of the sun.* Joshua 1:4
- *as soon as the sun was down.* Joshua 8:29
- *for He maketh His sun to rise.* Matthew 5:45
- *the time of the going down of the sun.* Joshua 10:27
- *toward the rising of the sun.* Joshua 12:1
- *as the sun when he goeth forth in his might.* Judges 5:31
- *before the sun was up.* Judges 8:13
- *as soon as the sun is up.* Judges 9:33
- *before the sun went down.* Judges 14:18
- *and the sun went down.* Judges 19:14
- *the sun went down.* II Samuel 2:24
- *till the sun be down.* II Samuel 3:35
- *when the sun riseth.* II Samuel 23:4
- *the going down of the sun.* I Kings 22:36
- *about the time of the sun going down.* II Chronicles 18:34
- *and called the earth from the rising of the sun unto the going down thereof.* Psalm 50:1
- *the sun ariseth.* Psalm 104:22
- *From the rising of the sun unto the going down of the same.* Psalm 113:3
- *from the rising of the sun.* Isaiah 41:25
- *from the rising of the sun.* Isaiah 45:6
- *from the rising of the sun.* Isaiah 59:19
- *Thy sun shall no more go down.* Isaiah 60:20
- *her sun is gone down while it was yet day.* Jeremiah 15:9
- *till the going down of the sun.* Daniel 6:14
- *when the sun did arise.* Jonah 4:8
- *and the sun shall go down.* Micah 3:6
- *when the sun ariseth.* Nahum 3:17
- *From the rising of the sun even unto the going down of the same.* Malachi 1:11
- *and when the sun was up.* Matthew 13:6
- *when the sun did set.* Mark 1:32
- *when the sun was up.* Mark 4:6
- *at the rising of the sun.* Mark 16:2
- *when the sun was setting.* Luke 4:40

- *let not the sun go down upon your wrath.* Ephesians 4:26
- *for the sun is no sooner risen.* James 1:11

The First, Second and Fourth Days: No Statement of Earth Motion

Genesis 1:1, Introduction to the Creation Week

1 In the beginning God created the heaven and the earth.

God's creation of the earth began on the First Day and was finished on the Sixth Day. His creation of the atmospheric and stellar heaven began on the Second Day, and was completed on the Fourth Day. Exodus 20:11 and 31:17 confirm that Genesis One is limited to seven literal days, and that there is no gap between verse one and the work of the First Day. Verse one therefore states what God accomplished in the Creation Week, with the details given on the successive days.

- *For in six days the LORD made heaven and earth, the sea, and all that in them is, and rested the seventh day.* Ex. 20:11.
- *for in six days the LORD made heaven and earth, and on the seventh day he rested, and was refreshed.* Ex. 31:17.

Genesis 1:2-5, First Day: The Earth Founded, Light Created
2 And the earth was without form, and void; and darkness was upon the face of the deep. And the Spirit of God moved upon the face of the waters.
3 And God said, let there be light: and there was light.
4 And God saw the light, that it was good: and God divided the light from the darkness.
5 And God called the light Day, and the darkness he called Night. And the evening and the morning were the first day.

The first day's work encompassed the initial or first stage of earth's creation, and the creation of the light to shine upon it. The only statement of motion on the first day is that *the Spirit of God moved upon the face of the waters.* It is natural to conclude that the light *prepared* in verse 3 (see Psalm 74:16; 104:2) continues this movement upon and around the earth, and thus dividing light from darkness and effecting day and night. The earth is not said to move or rotate beneath the Spirit of God. Consider the basic statement:

- *And the Spirit of God moved upon the face of the waters...And God said, Let there be light: and there was light.*

It is a natural to infer that the newly created light source continues the moving action of the Spirit of God, casting its rays *upon the face of the waters.* It is less natural as heliocentrism requires that this movement be transferred to the earth itself, and that the earth begins to rotate beneath and revolve around the light source. In these passages heliocentrism will always require further explanation and action than that stated. Nothing at all is said here about the earth rotating and revolving. As man is not created until verse 26, it can hardly be said that the description of Days One to Four is the language of appearance, or language from a human standpoint. No man was there to see it. This is a revelation *from God's standpoint.*

As the firmament is *the receptacle in which* the sun is placed (1:17), and as there was no firmament until the Second Day, this light which shone *out of darkness* on the First Day (II Cor. 4:6), and which likely also (as the Spirit of God) *moved upon the face of the deep*, may had been closer to the earth than the sun that was created on Day Four. Yet, the result was the same! The light of the First Day and the sun on the Fourth, each produced the same 24 hour day and night period for the earth. Thus while their distances from the earth were perhaps different, there basic motion and effect was the same. Both would have moved around the earth (from east to west), and not the earth around them.

Notice how Matthew Poole explains this:

> *There was light*; which was some bright and lucid body, peradventure like the fiery cloud in the wilderness, giving a small and imperfect light, successively moving over the several parts of the earth; and afterwards condensed, increased, perfected, and gathered together in the sun.

Noting again Gills comment:

> It is the opinion of Zanchius, and which is approved of by our countryman, Mr. Fuller, that it was a lucid body, or a small lucid cloud, which by its circular motion from east to west made day and night; perhaps somewhat like the cloudy pillar of fire that guided the Israelites in the wilderness, and had no doubt heat as well as light, (*Exposition of the Old Testament).*

There are some likely points of comparison with the movement of the pillar of fire in the wilderness.

- *And the LORD went before them by day in a pillar of a cloud, to lead them the way; and by night in a pillar of fire, to give them light; to go by day and night.* Exodus 13:21.

While the newly prepared light on the first day is to be distinguished from the Lord Himself, the statements of Psalm 104:2,5 should be reflected upon:

- *Who coverest thyself with light as with a garment: who stretchest out the heavens like a curtain... Who laid the foundations of the earth, that it should not be removed for ever.*

God on this First Day is not said to have "swung" the earth in orbit around the newly prepared light source, but rather *He hung the earth upon nothing*, Job 26:7. The earth was *stable*, I Chronicles. 16:30. It *cannot be moved*, Psalm 93:1. It became God's *footstool*, Isaiah 66:1. The only statement of motion on the First Day points much more naturally to that of the light source rather than the earth, nothing is said to indicate that this state was in any way changed on the Fourth Day.

With the phrase: *And the evening and the morning were the first day*, we have the beginning of time. Regarding which Thomas Strouse writes:

At the end of Day One all that God had created was the mass of darkened water, with the light moving around it (presumably form east to west). This movement initiated time, making the creation of time earth-centric, and therefore all time "earth-time." There was no heaven, and consequently the earth had no relationship with the un-created sun, moon or stars. God's creation was exclusively Geocentric. (*He Maketh His Sun to Rise*, p. 20).

As the phrase for time: *And the evening and the morning*, is repeated for each of the next five days, we expect no fundamental difference from the way time was initiated on the First Day. It is the light which moves and not the earth.

Genesis 1:6-8, Second Day: The Firmament Stretched Out

6 And God said, Let there be a firmament in the midst of the waters, and let it divide the waters from the waters.
7 And God made the firmament, and divided the waters which were under the firmament from the waters which were above the firmament: and it was so.
8 And God called the firmament Heaven. And the evening and the morning were the second day.

The command of God: *Let there be a firmament*, includes all that is visible above the earth, between it and the third heavens. It reaches as high as the place where the stars are fixed, *the firmament of heaven*, 1:14,15; and as low as the place where the birds fly, *the open firmament of heaven*, 1:20. Perhaps we are to assume that while the lower waters with the clouds were created on the First Day, the upper celestial waters which are the outer bound of the firmament were created on the Second Day.
This strange, unknowable, imperceptible firmament is shown on the Creation Week to be distinct from the sun, moon and stars that it contains. It was made on the Second Day, they on the Fourth Day; it therefore exists on its own right apart from them.

To speak of the firmament as an "expansion" or "space" falls far short, and is in complete opposition to the definition of the word. Whatever its properties, it does have substance (and this probably beyond our ability to comprehend. Indeed, one day of the Creation Week was *devoted entirely to its creation*. God on the Second Day did not merely create space and emptiness, but rather something so vast and powerful that it was capable of containing and holding in place an entire universe of stars and galaxies.

It is called the Firmament because:

1. It is a translation of the Hebrew word *raqiya*, and is based on *raqya* which the Bible uses of metal that is beaten or spread out.

- *And they did <u>beat</u> the gold into thin plates.* Exodus 39:3.
- *The workman melteth a graven image, and the goldsmith <u>spreadeth</u> it over with gold.* Isaiah 40:19.
- *Silver <u>spread</u> into plates is brought from Tarshish, and gold from Uphaz, the work of the workman, and of the hands of the founder.* Jeremiah 10:9.

2. The firmament is strong and powerful, and reflective as a molten looking glass.

- *Hast thou with him spread out the sky, which is strong, and as a molten looking glass?* Job 37:18.
- *Praise ye the LORD. Praise God in his sanctuary: praise him in the firmament of his power.* Psalm 150:1.

Of its reflective powers, Thomas Strouse writes:

Elihu likened the firmament to a strong, molten looking glass (Job 37:18) which suggests the reflective powers of the outer layer of water over the heaven. Presumably the waters above the firmament are the same as the "sea of glass like unto crystal" before the Lord's throne (cf. Revelation 4:6). God's throne (Psalm 11:4), which is in the third heaven, is "above the firmament" (Ezekiel 1:22-26). (*He Maketh His Sun to Rise*, p. 21).

3. The firmament is able to receive and support the placement of the sun, moon and stars.

- *And God made two great lights; the greater light to rule the day, and the lesser light to rule the night: he made the stars also. And God set them in the firmament of the heaven.* Genesis. 1:16,17.

4. The firmament is composed of stories. These likely refer to the galactic shells and walls of galaxies that are now known to encompass the heavens around the earth.

- *It is he that buildeth his stories in the heaven.* Amos 9:6.

5. The firmament supports upper waters. Indeed, this is the emphasis of the Second Day's account.

- *And God made the firmament, and divided the waters which were under the firmament from the waters which were above the firmament.* Genesis 1:7.
- *Praise him, ye heavens of heavens, and ye waters that be above the heavens.* Psalm 148:4.

Rainwater on the other hand is said to be from _in_ the heavens not *above* them.

- *When he uttereth his voice, there is a multitude of waters _in_ the heavens.* Jeremiah 51:16.

These upper waters likely refer to the sea of glass before the throne of God. Milton in referring to this long held view called these waters above the heavens, the "crystalline ocean." (Gill).

- *And before the throne there was a _sea of glass_ like unto crystal.* Revelation 4:6.
- *And I saw as it were a _sea of glass_ mingled with fire: and them that had gotten the victory over the beast...stand on the _sea of glass_, having the harps of God.* Revelation 15:2.

6. The firmament reaches even to the pavement of the holy city, and to the throne of God.

- *Then went up Moses, and Aaron, Nadab, and Abihu, and seventy of the elders of Israel: And they saw the God of Israel: and there was under his feet as it were a paved work of a sapphire stone, and as it were the body of heaven in his clearness.* Exodus 24:9,10.
- *And the likeness of the firmament upon the heads of the living creature was as the colour of the terrible crystal, stretched forth over their heads above_..._*

- *And above the firmament that was over their heads was the likeness of a throne, as the appearance of a sapphire stone: and upon the likeness of the throne was the likeness as the appearance of a man above upon it. Ezekiel. 1:22,26.*

7. The *stretched out* heavenly firmament in which the stars are placed provides a *tent* around the earth.

- *It is he that sitteth upon the circle of the earth, and the inhabitants thereof are as grasshoppers; that stretcheth out the heavens as a curtain, and spreadeth them out as a tent to dwell in. Isaiah 40:22.*

8. The light created on the First Day would be affected by the stretching out of the heavenly firmament on the Second Day.

Concerning this Thomas Strouse writes:

Since the Lord had provided the light during Day One, and the light continued in Day Two during which He created the heavens and stretched them out, presumably the light was affected by this stretching out process. If light is "stretched" as it moves through the stretched heavens, then there may not be any constant for the speed of light. Without a constant speed of light the heavens cannot be measured with "astronomical units" (A.U.), just as Jehovah God asserted saying:

- *Thus saith the LORD, which giveth the sun for a light by day, and the ordinances of the moon and of the stars for a light by night, which divideth the sea when the waves thereof roar; The LORD of hosts is his name: If those ordinances depart from before me, saith the LORD, then the seed of Israel also shall cease from being a nation before me for ever. Thus saith the LORD; If heaven above can be measured, and the foundations of the earth searched out beneath, I will also cast off all the seed of Israel for all that they have done, saith the LORD. Jeremiah 31:35-37, (pp. 22,23).*

9. The stretched out heavenly firmament will one day be *folded up* and *rolled together*.

- *and the heavens are the work of thy hands. They shall perish, but thou shalt endure: yea, all of them shall wax old like a garment; as a vesture shalt thou change them, and they shall be changed. Psalm 102:25,26.*
- *and the heavens are the works of thine hands: They shall perish; but thou remainest; and they all shall wax old as doth a garment; And as a vesture shalt thou fold them up, and they shall be changed: but thou art the same, and thy years shall not fail. Hebrews 1:10-12*
- *And all the host of heaven shall be dissolved, and the heavens shall be rolled together as a scroll: and all their host shall fall down, as the leaf falleth off from the vine, and as a falling fig from the fig tree. Isaiah 34:4.*
- *And the heaven departed as a scroll when it is rolled together. Revelation 6:14.*

10. The *founding* of the earth and the *stretching out* of the heavenly firmament are clearly distinguished from each other.

- *Of old hast thou laid the foundation of the earth: and the heavens are the work of thy hands.* Psalm 102:25.
- *And forgettest the LORD thy maker, that hath stretched forth the heavens, and laid the foundations of the earth.* Isaiah 51:13.
- *He hath made the earth by his power, he hath established the world by his wisdom, and hath stretched out the heavens by his discretion.* Jeremiah 10:12.
- *And, Thou, Lord, in the beginning hast laid the foundation of the earth; and the heavens are the works of thine hands.* Hebrews 1:10.

11. The creation of the firmament on the Second Day and its *garnishing* on the Fourth Day is also to be distinguished.

- *By his spirit he hath garnished the heavens; his hand hath formed the crooked serpent.* Job 26:13.
- *By the word of the LORD were the heavens made; and all the host of them by the breath of his mouth.* Psalm 33:6.

The firmament was the arena of Satan's and the angel's fall. According to early Jewish writers, this second day's work was not pronounced good; for it was on this day that Satan fell (Gill). Thus Satan is called *the prince of the power of the air*, Ephesians 2:2.

As the firmament has limits, waters above and waters below; and as the firmament *contains* the starry heavens, the universe is therefore finite. The notion that the universe is coterminous with God's infinity is false.

Modern Biblical exposition gives very little attention to the second day's work. It assumes *the language of appearance* and speaks of the firmament merely as an "expanse". It agrees with Einstein that space is empty space, without substance, or as Newton called it "ether". Biblical revelation indicates otherwise. In the firmament as with the Lord Himself, there is a *hiding of his power*, Hab. 3:4.

Genesis 1:14-19, Fourth Day: The Firmament Enlightened

14 And God said, Let there be lights in the firmament of the heaven to divide the day from the night; and let them be for signs, and for seasons, and for days, and years:
15 And let them be for lights in the firmament of the heaven to give light upon the earth: and it was so.
16 And God made two great lights; the greater light to rule the day, and the lesser light to rule the night: he made the stars also.
17 And God set them in the firmament of the heaven to give light upon the earth,
18 And to rule over the day and over the night, and to divide the light from the darkness: and God saw that it was good.
19 And the evening and the morning were the fourth day.

The Fourth Day is the middle day of the Creation Week, and with reference to the creation of light parallels the First Day. The record of the Fourth Day and especially verses 16 and 17 with 19, points convincingly to geocentricity.

- *And God made two great lights…he made the stars also.*
  And God set them in the firmament of the heaven to give light upon the earth…
  And the evening and the morning were the fourth day.

God made the sun, moon and starry host on the Fourth Day, and God set them in the firmament on the Fourth Day. There is no room in this statement for the sun, moon and stars merely *appearing* from behind the dispersing mists on the Fourth Day. They were *made* on this day. There is not the slightest hint of heliocentricism in any of these statements.

Malcolm Bowden, a leading British creationist has noted:

> To say that the sun and noon were created on the first day but only became visible on Day 4 is an unwarranted rendering of the scriptures. We can only conclude that it has been adopted by most Christians simply to preserve heliocentrism, as the earth could then circle the sun from the very first day of creation… The only acceptable interpretation of the Hebrew is that the sun did not exist until it was created on day four. The importance of this is seen when we ask the question: "what was the earth doing for the first three days of creation?" It could not have been circling a non-existent sun. When the sun was eventually created on the fourth day, did the earth suddenly have to jerk into action and circle the sun? The unlikelihood of this is obvious… (Malcolm Bowden, *True Science Agrees With The Bible,* p. 497).

The only stated purpose and effect of these lights is to give light upon the earth. They are said to *rule the day and night*; they are not said to rule the earth. They are said to *divide the light from darkness*. There is nothing said about any action or movement of the earth causing this division of light and darkness. One may choose to believe that the earth rotating caused this division of light and darkness, but such cannot be derived from the Biblical statements given. These statements teach the opposite. As with the First Day, so with the Fourth, the earth is not said to in any way contribute to the division of light and darkness, it is solely the work of the light on the First Day and the sun on the Fourth.

Consider again verse 14. *And God said, <u>Let there be lights</u> in the firmament of the heaven to divide the day from the night; and <u>let them be for</u>…days, and years.* This is specific. It is the sun and the moon that both produces the days and years and gives them their periodicity.

Three times the sun moon and stars of the Fourth Day are said to be placed by God in the firmament, (14,15,17). Biblical cosmology makes the earth anterior and primary, while the sun, moon and stars are secondary. They were made for the earth, not the earth for them. Conventional cosmology reverses this.

Of these Days Thomas Strouse concludes:

> The divine account of the creation of the heaven and earth through the first four days teaches an exclusively Geocentric perspective. This perspective is not phenomenological, because no one was standing on the earth at this time, but it is absolute. The Lord God, outside of His created heaven and earth, has spoken authoritatively about His creation of a Geocentric universe…. Never once does the Scripture state that the earth rotated relative to the sun, moon , stars or firmament. Never once does the Bible teach that the earth was

placed in the heavens to have motional interaction with the sun, moon, or stars. This *locus classicus* of all cosmological passages in Scripture teaches exclusively and consistently the Geocentric cosmology of a stationary earth and a revolving firmament with sun, moon, and stars. (p. 26).

Occam's Razor (also Ockham) is a maxim attributed to William of Ockham (died 1349?). It states that the preferred theory is that which has to make the fewest assumptions in explaining all of the relevant evidence or data. Certainly, if we limit ourselves to the Genesis reading of Days One, Two and Four, it is geocentricity that makes the fewer assumptions, and which provides the natural conclusion. The same will be found to be true if Occam's Razor is applied to each of the other geocentric passages of the Bible.

An Examination of 50 Selected Passages

Genesis 28:11-13

11 And he lighted upon a certain place, and tarried there all night, because the sun was set; and he took of the stones of that place, and put them for his pillows, and lay down in that place to sleep.
12 And he dreamed, and behold a ladder set up on the earth, and the top of it reached to heaven: and behold the angels of God ascending and descending on it.
13 And, behold, the LORD stood above it, and said, I am the LORD God of Abraham thy father, and the God of Isaac: the land whereon thou liest, to thee will I give it, and to thy seed;

The ladder (a type of Christ, John 1:51) connects heaven to earth. As with Isaiah 66:1, the heaven is my throne, and the earth is my footstool, the earth is stationary with reference to the throne of God. There is no thought here of a rotating and revolving earth. The earth is not moving beneath the ladder.

This is also one of the Bibles ascending and descending passages. See at Ephesians 4:8-10 for a list of seventeen of these passages. They show that there is a direct rather than a circuitous link between the earth and the Throne of God in Heaven, and as such demonstrate geocentricity.

Joshua 10:12-14

12 Then spake Joshua to the LORD in the day when the LORD delivered up the Amorites before the children of Israel, and he said in the sight of Israel, Sun, stand thou still upon Gibeon; and thou, Moon, in the valley of Ajalon.
13 And the sun stood still, and the moon stayed, until the people had avenged themselves upon their enemies. Is not this written in the book of Jasher? So the sun stood still in the midst of heaven, and hasted not to go down about a whole day.
14 And there was no day like that before it or after it, which the LORD hearkened unto the voice of a man: for the LORD fought for Israel.

In today's cosmology, the sun is stationary with reference to the earth and the moon is in motion, but here both are said to be moving, and both are made to stand still. Therefore by this reasoning the statement that the moon stayed is correct, but that the sun stood still is incorrect. How can it stand still if it is not moving? How can there be truth and false hood in two immediately parallel statements? Further, as heliocentrism requires that the earth would have to cease its rotational movement; it is to be noted that nothing in this account is said of the earth at all. Every statement concerns the movement of the sun and moon. For the earth to suddenly or even gradually stop its rotation, a further miracle would be required to prevent it being overwhelmed by catastrophe.

Many believe that for convenience, as men did not then know that the earth rotated, the Holy Spirit is presenting this miracle in the language of appearance rather than actuality. The Bible says the sun stood still, but actually "it was the earth that stood still". This would set a serious precedent: i.e. that the Bible from time to time presents things only as they appear to be, not as they really are.
James Hanson notes that even if it were the earth rather than the sun that stood still, this would still not solve the problem this passage presents for heliocentricity.

> The Bible states that the sun and moon stood still, that is, they did not move. If, however, the earth stopped rotating, or if it flipped its axis; and if Copernicus were correct, then there is still the residual motion of earth about the sun, which would cause the sun to move through twice its diameter during Joshua's long day. Even worse is the case for the moon, for stopping the earth in no way stops the moon's independent motion about the earth, which, in one day, amounts to 13 degrees or a movement of about 26 lunar diameters. (*The Bible and Geocentricity*, p. 47).

The event here is to be taken in the same literal manner as Christ walking on the water, the plagues of Egypt, the crossing of the Red Sea and countless other miracles. As Matthew Henry comments: "at the word of Joshua, the sun stopped immediately".
This event is also recorded in Job 9:7 and Habakkuk 3:11.

Judges 5:20

"*They fought from heaven; the stars in their courses fought against Sisera.*"

Mesillah (courses) is usually translated "highway", i.e. highways in OT Israel, but it is never said that the earth itself is on a mesillah. Compare the sun's circuit (Psalm 19:6).

Judges 5:31

"*So let all thine enemies perish, O LORD: but let them that love him be as the sun when he goeth forth in his might.*"

"*As a strong man to run a race,*" Psalm 19:5. We do not read in Scripture of the earth going forth.

I Samuel 2:8

"...for the pillars of the earth are the LORD'S, and he hath set the world upon them."

A rotating, revolving earth set upon pillars is a contradiction. These pillars find further expression and definition in Hebrews 1:3...upholding all things by the word of his power.

II Kings 20:9-11

9 And Isaiah said, This sign shalt thou have of the LORD, that the LORD will do the thing that he hath spoken: shall the shadow go forward ten degrees, or go back ten degrees?
10 And Hezekiah answered, It is a light thing for the shadow to go down ten degrees: nay, but let the shadow return backward ten degrees.
11 And Isaiah the prophet cried unto the LORD: and he brought the shadow ten degrees backward, by which it had gone down in the dial of Ahaz.

Was this action of the shadow caused by the earth reversing its rotation, or by the sun reversing its revolution around a stationary earth? Isaiah 38:8 says it was the sun that returned. "Whether this retrograde motion of the sun was gradual or per salutm –suddenly - whether it went back at the same pace that it used to go forward, which would make the day ten hours longer than usual - or whether it darted back on a sudden, and, after continuing a little while, was restored again to it usual place, so that no change was made in the state of the heavenly bodies (as the learned bishop Patrick thinks) - we are not told." Matthew Henry.

I Chronicles 16:30,31

30 Fear before him, all the earth: the world also shall be stable, that it be not moved.
31 Let the heavens be glad, and let the earth rejoice: and let men say among the nations, The LORD reigneth.

It is only in times of judgement, especially that of the last days, that the earth is said to move (Job 9:6; Psalm 99:1; Isaiah 13:13; 24:19,20; Revelation 20:11). At all other times it is stable and not moved. Compare Psalm 96:10.

Job 9:6-8

6 Which shaketh the earth out of her place, and the pillars thereof tremble.
7 Which commandeth the sun, and it riseth not; and sealeth up the stars.
8 Which alone spreadeth out the heavens, and treadeth upon the waves of the sea.

The earth has a *place*, not a *path*. Not *courses*, Judges 5:20. Not a *circuit*, Psalm 19:6. Not a *going forth*, Judges 5:39. The earth is moved from her *place* only in times of judgement. The command in verse 7 is specifically directed to the sun, nothing is said of God commanding the earth in its rotational movement.

Job 22:14

Thick clouds are a covering to him, and that he seeth not; and he walketh in the circuit of heaven.

The Hebrew word *chug* is translated "circuit", "circle" and "compass". The sun (Psalm 19:6), and the heavens have a *circuit* in which they move around the earth. Compare *the stars in their courses*, Judges 5:20. We do not read of the earth having a *circuit*.

Job 26:7

He stretcheth out the north over the empty place, and <u>hangeth the earth upon nothing</u>.

The earth is not said to hang from the sun in a gravitational orbit, but *upon nothing*. This is in contrast to Newton and Einstein who insist that there must always be some center of mass, some concentration of material upon which gravitation must be "fastened". (Gerardus Bouw, *Geocentricity*, p. 139). Christ *upholds all things by the word of his power*, Hebrews 1:3. "The art of man could not hang a feather upon nothing, yet divine wisdom hangs the whole world so." *Matthew Henry*.

Note that this verse also teaches that in God's creation there is an *absolute north*.

Job 37:18

Hast thou with him spread out the sky, <u>which is strong</u>, and <u>as a molten looking glass</u>?

So *strong* that that the Second Day was given solely to *its* creation. So *strong* that it could receive and support the placement of the sun, moon and stars, (Genesis 1:14-17). So *strong* that it can be referred to as the *firmament of his power*, Psalms 150:1. The firmament has properties that are incomprehensible to us. "When we look up to heaven above we should remember it is a mirror or looking-glass, not to show us our own faces, but to be a faint representation of the purity, dignity, and brightness of the upper world and its glorious inhabitants." *Matthew Henry*.

Job 38:4-7

4 Where wast thou when <u>I laid the foundations of the earth</u>? declare, if thou hast understanding.
5 Who hath laid the measures thereof, if thou knowest? or who hath stretched the line upon it?
6 Whereupon are the <u>foundations</u> thereof fastened? or who <u>laid the corner stone</u> thereof;
7 When the morning stars sang together, and all the sons of God shouted for joy?

It is far more natural and reasonable to equate an earth at rest with *foundations*, than one that is rotating, tilting and revolving.

Job 38:12-14

12 Hast thou commanded the morning since thy days; and <u>caused the dayspring to know his place</u>;
13 That it might take hold of the ends of the earth, that the wicked might be shaken out of it?
14 It is <u>turned as clay to the seal</u>; and they stand as a garment.
Referring to "*turned* " in verse 14, some have said this refers to the turning of the earth and therefore a (sole!) passage has at last been found which supports heliocentricity.

It does not! It is the dayspring – the sun – *which knows his place*, and therefore moves. When its light beams *take hold on the ends of the earth*, the effect is as complete and prevailing as clay filling the impression of a seal. As the clay moves upward filling completely all of the crevices, so in the same irresistible way the earth is turned up exposing the wicked to the light of the sun (v 13). It is much like a farmer, turning up the soil, exposing rocks, worms etc. In the coming Day of the Lord there will be no hiding place! Revelation 6:16.

Job 38:31-33

31 Canst thou <u>bind</u> the sweet influences of Pleiades, or <u>loose</u> the bands of Orion?
32 Canst thou <u>bring forth</u> Mazzaroth in his season? or canst thou <u>guide</u> Arcturus with his sons?
33 Knowest thou the ordinances of heaven? canst thou set the dominion thereof in the earth?

Job is challenged in these verses as to his inability to control the movements of the constellations. Can he *bind* Pleiades? *Loose* Orion? *Guide* Arcturus? Can he control their movements from the earth (*verse 33*)?

Can Job *bring forth Massaroth in his season*? According to Bullinger, *Massaroth* refers to the yearly unfolding of the twelve signs of the Zodiac, (*The Witness of the Stars*, p.8). Satan has been successful in perverting the testimony of the stars. Secular astronomy and heathen astrology has all but obliterated their ancient message of Biblical truth.

Psalm 19:1-6

1 The heavens declare the glory of God; and <u>the firmament sheweth his handywork</u>.
2 Day unto day uttereth speech, and night unto night sheweth knowledge.
3 There is no speech nor language, where their voice is not heard.
4 Their line is gone out through all the earth, and their words to the end of the world. In them hath <u>he set a tabernacle for the sun</u>,
5 Which is <u>as a bridegroom coming out of his chamber, and rejoiceth as a strong man to run a race</u>.
6 <u>His going forth</u> is from the end of the heaven, and <u>his circuit</u> unto the ends of it: and there is nothing hid from the heat thereof.

Four statements are here made about solar motion. The sun is spoken of as: *coming out*, *running a race*, *going forth*, and having a *circuit*. Nothing similar is said in any passage of Scripture about the movement of the earth.

Of the sixth verse Gerardus Bouw writes:

> The sixth verse is eminently Christological. The motion of the sun is there linked to the emergence of the bridegroom…The Authorized Bible starts the verse with the personal pronoun, "his", thus reinforcing the type to the bridegroom and also the Christology of the verse. Modern versions start this verse with "its" and thus deny the person of Christ as being evident in this verse and so also deny that the sun is a type of Christ in this passage. The sun's circuit (verse 6) takes it around the zodiac, yearly tracing the gospel as told in the stars: starting from the nativity (Virgo) to the sacrificial death, resurrection, and final triumph as the Lion of Judah which is reflected in the constellation of Leo, the lion. (Gerardus Bouw, *Geocentricity,* pp. 83,84).

It is said that verse six must refer to the sun's galactic circuit in the Milky Way, as the sun's circuit around the earth is too small in comparison to the size of the universe. However, by the same comparison, a galactic circuit is not much larger. Further, as by definition, a circuit must have a closed and repeated path, a galactic "circuit" for the sun will not meet again at the same point, and will certainly not begin to complete a revolution around a galactic centre within the creationist time frame. Thus, only in a geocentric system can the sun's motion be described in terms of a circuit.

Verse 6 coupled with passages like Revelation 6:13 (See Note) indicate that the universe is not as large as thought today and is more in line with what previous ages considered the size of the

celestial heavens to be. As discussed later, what we see of the stars by the naked eye and what we see of them through the telescope is quite surprising. It certainly surprised Galileo!

The concluding verse of Psalm 19 is pertinent as a summary to the geocentric aspects of this Psalm.

- *Let the words of my mouth, and the meditation of my heart, be acceptable in thy sight, O LORD, my strength, and my redeemer.19:14.*
- *Because they regard not the works of the LORD, nor the operation of his hands, he shall destroy them, and not build them up. Psalm 28:5.*

   "In order that the Creationist's words and meditations 'be acceptable' in the Lord's sight, he must say and think what God has revealed through nature and Scripture." (Strouse, p. 29).

Psalm 33:6-9

6 By the word of the LORD were the heavens made; and all the host of them by the breath of his mouth.
7 He gathereth the waters of the sea together as an heap: he layeth up the depth in storehouses.
8 Let all the earth fear the LORD: let all the inhabitants of the world stand in awe of him.
9 For he spake, and it was done; he commanded, and it stood fast.
The words, *it stood fast (amad)*, in verse 9 summarizes God's creative works during the Creation Week. It must refer to the earth itself, and especially so as the earth was the subject of the great majority of creative actions during the First Week.
He *spake...commanded*, compare these *Ten Commandments* in Genesis One: (1:3,6,9,11,14,20,24,26,28,29).

Psalm 50:1

The mighty God, even the LORD, hath spoken, and called the earth from the rising of the sun unto the going down thereof.

God calls to the earth beneath a sun that has a *rising* and a *going down*. It is always stated this way in Scripture. It is the sun that moves, the earth remains stationary. If it were the opposite, why do not once read of an example?

Concerning this passage Thomas Strouse says:

   "The earth is the fixed focal point around which all cosmic movement revolves." (p. 23).

Psalm 74:16

The day is thine, the night also is thine: thou hast prepared the light and the sun.

The *light* on the First Day and the *sun* on the Fourth Day are both described in Genesis One as being secondary and subservient to the earth. We have shown there that they both share the same kind of motion relative to the stationary earth.

Psalm 78:69

And he built his sanctuary like high palaces, like <u>the earth which he hath established for ever</u>.

The Hebrew for "established" is yasad, and means, "to found," "to lay a foundation," and is thus frequently translated, (Young's Concordance). As His sanctuary is not moveable, the same would naturally apply to the earth. Compare Psalms 93:1; 96:10; 119:90.

Psalm 93:1,2

1 The LORD reigneth, he is clothed with majesty; the LORD is clothed with strength, wherewith he hath girded himself: <u>the world also is stablished, that it cannot be moved</u>.
2 <u>Thy throne is established of old</u>: thou art from everlasting.

The passage says that the world cannot be moved. We therefore conclude that it is not moving. One must go to considerable lengths to explain how an earth that is rotating and revolving is somehow "not moving". One attempt is to say that it is the orbit rather than the world itself that cannot be moved. We would then, however, expect a different word or phrase than "moved". Perhaps: "moved from its path", or "changed", or "deflected"; certainly not the single word "moved." Notice also that the *world* is here paralleled with the *throne* of God, which does not move. The same Hebrew word (*kun* = established) is used for both. "Though He has hanged the world upon nothing (Job 26:7), yet it cannot be moved". *Matthew Henry.*

Psalm 99:1

The LORD reigneth; let the people tremble: he sitteth between the cherubims; <u>let the earth be moved</u>.

It is only in times of judgement, especially that of the last days, that the earth is said to *be moved* (I Chronicles 16:30,31; Job 9:6; Isaiah 13:13; 24:19,20; Revelation 20:11). At all other times *it cannot be moved,* Psalm 93:1.

Psalm 102:25

Of old hast thou <u>laid the foundation of the earth</u>: and the heavens are the work of thy hands.

We have listed 21 passages that speak of the *foundations* of the earth. See for example Job 38:4; Psalm 104:5; Jeremiah 31:37; Micah 6:2; Hebrews 1:8. Compare *pillars*
I Samuel 2:8. One never thinks of a foundation in terms of an object that rotates, tilts and revolves.

Psalm 104:5

Who <u>laid the foundations of the earth</u>, that it should not be removed for ever.

Again, *foundations* speak of the fixity of a *place*, not the fixity of a *path*.

Psalm 104:19

He appointed the moon for seasons: <u>the sun knoweth his going down</u>.

An impossible concept to reconcile with heliocentricity! How could the sun know *its going down* if it is not going down? If it is motionless? If the earth is turning beneath the sun? To speak of this as poetic language ignores the fact that the first half of the verse is clearly not poetic. Both the moon and the sun observe exactly the *appointments* of their Creator. See Matthew Henry on this verse.

Psalm 119:89,90

89 For ever, O LORD, <u>thy word is settled</u> in heaven.
90 Thy faithfulness is unto all generations: <u>thou hast established the earth, and it abideth</u>.

The fixedness of the earth is equated with the fixedness of the Scriptures. *Amad* (abideth) means: "to stand," "to stand still," "to remain," (*Young's Concordance*).

Proverbs 3:19

The LORD by wisdom hath <u>founded the earth</u>; by understanding hath he established the heavens.

Yasad (founded) means, "to lay a foundation"; while *established* for the heavens is *kun*, "to form," "prepare," "establish," (*Young's Concordance*).

Proverbs 8:27

When he prepared the heavens, I was there: <u>when he set a compass</u> upon the face of the depth.

In their creation, the point of the compass was placed not in the heavens but upon the watery earth. As Matthew Henry says on this verse:

> He was no less active when, on the second day, he stretched out the firmament, the vast expanse, and *set* that as *a compass upon the face of the depth*, surrounded it on all sides with that canopy, that curtain. Or it may refer to the exact order and method with which God framed all the parts of the universe, as the workman marks out his work with his line and compasses. The work in nothing varied from the plan of it formed in the eternal mind.

Ecclesiastes 1:4-7

4 One generation passeth away, and another generation cometh: but <u>the earth abideth</u> for ever.

5 The sun also <u>ariseth</u>, and the sun <u>goeth down</u>, and <u>hasteth</u> to his place where he arose.

6 The wind <u>goeth</u> toward the south, and <u>turneth</u> about unto the north; it <u>whirleth</u> about continually, and the wind <u>returneth</u> again according to his circuits.

7 All the rivers <u>run</u> into the sea; yet the sea is not full; unto the place from whence the rivers come, thither they <u>return.</u>

In contrast to the *abiding earth* (amad = *to stand, stand still, remain*), *four* statements are made of the motion of the wind (*goeth, turneth, whirleth, returneth*), two are made of rivers (*run, return*), and three are made of the sun's movements (*ariseth, goeth down, hasteth to the place where he arose*). As the wind and rivers move relative to the earth, this passage declares that the sun does likewise. Only one, not two, hermeneutical principles can be allowed in this brief comparison. Actuality is not mingled here with the language of appearance. The sixteen words of motion in this passage are all actual.

Isaiah 13:10

For the stars of heaven and the constellations thereof shall not give their light: <u>the sun shall be darkened in his going forth</u>, and the moon shall not cause her light to shine.

As in Judges 5:31 and Psalm 19:5,6, it is once again stated that the *sun goes forth*. And here, in its going forth it will be darkened. Two actions are therefore attributed to the sun alone, a darkening and a going forth. It is not one action of the sun, a darkening, and another of the earth, a rotation.

Isaiah 13:13

Therefore I will shake the heavens, and <u>the earth shall remove out of her place</u>, in the wrath of the LORD of hosts, and in the day of his fierce anger.

Only in times of judgement (mainly that of the last days) is the earth said to move. Compare Psalms 82:5; 99:1; Isaiah 24:19,20. Notice again, the earth is removed out of her *place*. Again we note that earth has a *place* not a *path*, Job 9:6.

Isaiah 24:19,20

19 The earth is utterly broken down, the earth is clean dissolved, <u>the earth is moved exceedingly</u>.
20 The earth shall reel to and fro like a drunkard, and shall be <u>removed</u> like a cottage; and the transgression thereof shall be heavy upon it; and it shall fall, and not rise again.

There will be violent movement of the earth during the coming Great Tribulation, and with this verse likely looking beyond to Revelation 20:11.

- *And I saw a great white throne, and him that sat on it, from whose face the earth and the heaven fled away; and there was found no place for them.*

Isaiah 38:7,8

7 And this shall be a sign unto thee from the LORD, that the LORD will do this thing that he hath spoken; 8 Behold, <u>I will bring again the shadow</u> of the degrees, which is gone down in the sun dial of Ahaz, ten degrees backward. <u>So the sun returned ten degrees</u>, by which degrees it was gone down.

Thus it was the sun, and not only the shadow that returned, II Kings 20:11. In Joshua 10:13 *the sun stood still*; here the sun reverses its motion. The sun is faithful to its *appointments* (Psalm 104:19). "*The sun is a faithful measurer of time, and rejoices as a strong man to run a race; but he that set that clock a going can set it back when he pleases, and make it to return; for the Father of all lights is the director of them.*" *Matthew Henry.*

Isaiah 40:26

Lift up your eyes on high, and behold who hath created these things, <u>that bringeth out their host by number</u>: he calleth them all by names by the greatness of his might, for that he is strong in power; not one faileth.

We are called to behold the majesty of Lord's power as he *brings out* the starry host in their nightly circuit across the darkened sky. This is a further of illustration of Judges 5:20, the *stars in their courses*. Compare the sun's *circuit* (Psalm 19:6). On the Fourth Day of the Creation Week the starry host was *stretched out* (Job 26:7), now nightly we see them *brought out*.

Isaiah 48:13

Mine hand also hath <u>laid the foundation of the earth</u>, and my right hand hath <u>spanned the heavens</u>: when I call unto them, they stand up together.

The usual terminology of creation is that of the heavens being *stretched out* and the earth *founded*. See Jeremiah 10:12. This clearly points to *geo* rather than *helio* - centricity.

Isaiah 66:1

Thus saith the LORD, The heaven is my throne, and <u>the earth is my footstool</u>: where is the house that ye build unto me? and where is the place of my rest?

As with Jacob's ladder (Genesis 28), there is here a stationary throne in heaven joined to a stationary earth below. One does not expect to see a rotating, tilting and revolving footstool. Nor would one expect such a footstool to be a *place of rest*. Note also

Acts 7:49.

- *Heaven is my throne, and <u>earth is my footstool</u>: what house will ye build me? saith the Lord: or what is <u>the place of my rest</u>?*

Jeremiah 10:12

He hath made the earth by his power, he hath established the world by his wisdom, and hath stretched out the heavens by his discretion.

The word *establish* here is *kun* (= form, prepare, establish), rather than the frequently used *yasad* (= to lay a foundation). This passage gives another contrasting example of the creation of earth with that of the heavens. Compare the *stretching out* of the heavens with their *rolling up*, Isaiah 34:4; Hebrews 1:12. The language is geocentric.

The collection of red shift and other data over the past 40 years indicates the existence of astronomical "shells" around the earth. See below on Amos 9:6.

Amos 5:7,8

7 Ye who turn judgment to wormwood, and leave off righteousness in the earth,
8 Seek him that maketh the seven stars and Orion, and turneth the shadow of death into the morning, and maketh the day dark with night: that calleth for the waters of the sea, and poureth them out upon the face of the earth: The LORD is his name:
As with the actions of the First and Fourth Days of Creation, and the actions described below in Amos 8:9, along with the actions of numerous other passages, when God *turneth the shadow of death into the morning, and maketh the day dark with night*, it is an action from without affecting the earth, and not of the earth's rotation affecting itself.

Amos 8:9

And it shall come to pass in that day, saith the Lord GOD, that I will cause the sun to go down at noon, and I will darken the earth in the clear day.

This likely refers to the same action on the sun described in Revelation 8:12

- *and the third part of the sun was smitten…and the day shone not for a third part of it.*

God's action is specifically stated to be applied to the sun, there is no indication here of action being applied to the earth. Nothing is said of God speeding up the rotation of the earth.

Amos 9:6

It is he that buildeth his stories in the heaven, and hath founded his troop in the earth; he that calleth for the waters of the sea, and poureth them out upon the face of the earth: The LORD is his name.

As the Lord GOD of Hosts (9:5), He is in complete control of His creation whether it be the upper reaches of the heavens or the lower parts - the earth. Regarding the upper parts, recent discoveries have demonstrated the existence of galactic and other types of astronomical "shells" around the earth. This appears to lead inescapably to the conclusion that the earth is at the centre!

The famous astronomer Edwin Hubble said that this dilemma was "intolerable". At the Mount Palomar observatory in the 1930s and 40s, Hubble observed consistent evidence that pointed to the "ancient conception of a central earth." (*The Observational Approach to Cosmology*, pp. 50-58).

Astronomer W. G. Tifft found that the red shift of various galaxies was all distributed at specific spherical distances from earth. (*Astrophysical Journal* 287: pp. 492-502).

Astrophysicist J. I. Katz declared: "the distribution of gamma-ray burst sources in space is a sphere or spherical shell with us at the center". (*The Biggest Bangs, The Mystery of Gamma-Ray Bursts*, pp. 90-91).

The same is true of energy sources in deep space known as quasars (quasi-stellar radio sources). Astrophysicist Y. P. Varshni found that they "are arranged in 57 spherical shells with the earth at the center". He concluded: "The earth is indeed the center of the Universe…These shells would disappear if viewed from another galaxy". (*Astrophysics and Space Science*, 43:(1), pp. 3,8).

Indeed, *It is he that <u>buildeth his stories in the heavens</u>. Amos 9:6.*

Habakkuk 3:11

10 The mountains saw thee, and they trembled: the overflowing of the water passed by: the deep uttered his voice, and lifted up his hands on high.
11 <u>The sun and moon stood still in their habitation</u>: at the light of thine arrows they went, and at the shining of thy glittering spear.

In this further reference to Joshua's long day, *the sun and moon stood still in their habitation*, that is, in the heavens. The earth was not the place where the passage says motion was suspended. It was in the sphere of the heavens where *the sun and the moon stood still*.

Zechariah 12:1

The burden of the word of the LORD for Israel, saith the LORD, which <u>stretcheth forth the heavens</u>, and <u>layeth the foundation of the earth</u>, and formeth the spirit of man within him.

Why is this repeated statement of the laying the foundation of the earth not made of the sun, moon or stars? Why this continual contrast? The heavens are *stretched out* but the earth is *laid as a foundation*. This is a clear demonstration of geocentricity.

Malachi 1:11 and 4:2

1:11 for from <u>the rising of the sun</u> even unto the going down of the same my name shall be great among the Gentiles;
4:2 But unto you that fear my name <u>shall the Sun of righteousness arise</u> with healing in his wings; and ye shall go forth, and grow up as calves of the stall.

Appearing in proximity, both "risings" must convey the same thought. Both are actual. As the *Sun* (Christ) rises in 4:2, so does also the *sun* in 1:11.

Christ's Coming is likened and typified elsewhere by the movement of the sun.

- Which is as a bridegroom coming out of his chamber, and rejoiceth as a strong man to run a race. Psalm 19:5.
- *The people which sat in darkness saw great light; and to them which sat in the region and shadow of death light is sprung up. Matthew 4:16.*
- *Through the tender mercy of our God; whereby the dayspring from on high hath visited us, To give light to them that sit in darkness and in the shadow of death, to guide our feet into the way of peace. Luke 1:78, 79.*

Matthew 5:45

That ye may be the children of your Father which is in heaven: for <u>he maketh his sun to rise</u> on the evil and on the good, and sendeth rain on the just and on the unjust.

He maketh his sun to rise (not merely *to shine*) is a statement of action being exercised upon the sun itself. We would expect this to convey the same literal meaning as, He *sendeth the rain*. The *Father* is the subject; *maketh to rise*, and *sendeth* are the verbs; *sun* and *rain* are the objects of the verbs. The Fathers actions on both objects must be viewed in the same literal manner. The first action in this coupled statement could not be the "language of appearance", if the second is an actual statement of fact.

Mark 16:2,6

2 And very early in the morning the first day of the week, they came unto the sepulchre at the <u>rising of the sun</u>.
6 And he saith unto them, Be not affrighted: Ye seek Jesus of Nazareth, which was crucified: <u>he is risen</u>; he is not here: behold the place where they laid him.
As in Malachi 1:11 and 4:2 both the Saviour and the sun rose actually. *Rising* and *risen* have the same relative meaning. In Scripture the rising of the sun is frequently found in immediate context with a statement of actual motion. *Both* must be actual.

Acts 7:49

Heaven is my throne, and <u>earth is my footstool</u>: what house will ye build me? saith the Lord: or what is the place of my rest?

A *house* (Solomon's Temple) was to be built. This would be God's *rest* on His *footstool* the *earth*. This is incongruous if earth (unlike the throne in heaven) is in multi-directional motion.

Ephesians 4:8-10
8 Wherefore he saith, When <u>he ascended up on high</u>, he led captivity captive, and gave gifts unto men.
9 (Now that he ascended, what is it but that he also <u>descended first into the lower parts of the earth</u>?

10 He that descended is the same also that <u>ascended up far above all heavens</u>, that he might fill all things.)

The ascending and descending passages of the Bible are geocentric.

- Elijah *went up by a whirlwind into heaven*. II Kings 4:11.
- After their appearance to the shepherds, *the angels were gone away from them into heaven*. Luke 2:15.
- At Christ's ascension, *he was received up into heaven, and sat on the right hand of God*. Mark 16:19; *And... while he blessed them, he was parted from them, and carried up into heaven*. Luke 24:51.
- At the Rapture, *the Lord himself shall descend from* heaven. I Thess. 4:16.
- Shortly before Christ's Return John *saw another mighty angel come down from heaven*. Rev. 10:1.
- The Two Witnesses are told to, *Come up hither. And they ascended up to heaven in a cloud*. Rev.11:12.
- At Christ's Return, the book of Micah describes: *For, behold, the LORD cometh forth out of his place, and will come down, and tread upon the high places of the earth*. Micah 1:3.

To these we could add:

- *Then the LORD rained upon Sodom and upon Gomorrah brimstone and fire from the LORD out of heaven*. Gen. 19:24.
- *For it came to pass, when the flame went up toward heaven from off the altar, that the angel of the LORD ascended in the flame of the altar*. Judges 13:20.
- *If I ascend up into heaven, thou art there: if I make my bed in hell, behold, thou art there*. Psa. 139:8.
- *Who hath ascended up into heaven, or descended*? Prov. 30:4.
- *And no man hath ascended up to heaven, but he that came down from heaven, even the Son of man which is in heaven*. John 3:13.
- *that of the fruit of his loins, according to the flesh, he would raise up Christ to sit on his throne*. Acts 2:30.
- *Say not in thine heart, Who shall ascend into heaven? (that is, to bring Christ down from above:) Or, Who shall descend into the deep? (that is, to bring up Christ again from the dead)*. Rom. 10:6,7.
- *And the smoke of the incense, which came with the prayers of the saints, ascended up before God out of the angel's hand. And the angel took the censer, and filled it with fire of the altar, and cast it into the earth*. Rev. 8:4,5.

As with Jacob's ladder (Gen. 28), the Bible declares that there is a direct rather than a circuitous link between the earth and the Throne of God in Heaven.

Hebrews 1:10

And, Thou, Lord, in the beginning hast laid the foundation of the earth; and the heavens are the works of thine hands:

Once again we see this phrase. Few expressions could so completely preclude the thought of motion than the laying of a foundation.

James 1:17

Every good gift and every perfect gift is from above, and cometh down from the Father of lights, with whom is no variableness, neither shadow of turning.

In comparison with other lights (Sun, Moon, Stars) where there *is* variableness and shadow of turning, with God there *is no variableness, neither shadow of turning*. There is directness between God and his dealings with the earth. (See Thomas Strouse, "James and Astronomy," *The Biblical Astronomer*, Fall 2005).

Revelation 6:13,14

13 And the stars of heaven fell unto the earth, even as a fig tree casteth her untimely figs, when she is shaken of a mighty wind
14 And the heaven departed as a scroll when it is rolled together; and every mountain and island were moved out of their places.

This passage is geocentric. In Genesis 1, the earth is created on the First Day, and is therefore distinct from the firmament created on the Second Day, and from the stars created and set in the firmament on the Fourth Day. This same geocentric distinctiveness is seen in the celestial judgements of the Tribulation. The stars fall upon the earth. The overhead heavenly canopy is rolled up.

- *And the stars of heaven shall fall, and the powers that are in heaven shall be shaken.* Mark 13:25
- *And all the host of heaven shall be dissolved, and the heavens shall be rolled together as a scroll: and all their host shall fall down, as the leaf falleth off from the vine, and as a falling fig from the fig tree.* Isaiah 34:4.

Revelation 6:13 is likely to be one of the most *disbelieved* verses in the Bible. How could stars fall on to the earth! There is the surprising fact that whether with the naked eye or the most powerful telescopes, stars only and always appear as points of light. Nor when viewed through a telescope do we see them enlarged as when viewing for example the planets. This was a surprise to Galileo, and the anomaly remains. There is something wonderfully strange about the stars!

- *Praise ye him, sun and moon: praise him, all ye stars of light.* Psalm 148:3.

Revelation 8:12

And the fourth angel sounded, and the third part of the sun was smitten, and the third part of the moon, and the third part of the stars; so as the third part of them was darkened, and the day shone not for a third part of it, and the night likewise.

It is *difficult* to conceive of these judgements during the Tribulation Period when:

- *the sun shall be darkened, and the moon shall not give her light, and the stars shall fall from heaven, and the powers of the heavens shall be shaken.* Matthew 24:29.

If one considers carefully what is stated in Revelation 8:12, it is *impossible* to conceive of these events taking place if the earth is spinning around the sun. Here it is the *sun* that is said to be *smitten*, not the earth's rotation. The passage tells that men will look up to see a *smitten sun* that does not shine for a third part of the day (*for a third part of it*), and the third part of *the night likewise* will be moonless and starless.

Conclusion

Therefore, except in the judgements of the last days (Isa. 24:20), there appears to be no passage in the Bible that indicate the earth is in motion. All movement is by the sun, moon and stars. In Psalm 104:19 God *appointed the moon for seasons: <u>the sun knoweth his going down</u>*. This is the way it is *always* presented. If it were the opposite, would we not expect the Bible to say so *at least once*!

Beginning with Genesis One and then on to fifty selected passages, the Bible shows that the earth has a *place* rather than a *path*. It is not moving through the cosmos. In addition more than one hundred additional passages have been listed. The cumulative effect is convincing, and especially so when *nothing* in Scripture can be gathered for the other side. It is for this reason that Bible believers in that previous day were loath to surrender to heliocentricity. They considered that the Scriptures themselves were being surrendered. They were right! And, it was a surrender that prepared the way for the next great capitulation: *Darwinism*!

It is the Scriptures where the quest for knowledge must be centered. In the subject before us, a kind of peer pressure has caused men, including many creationists, to look elsewhere and ignore the consistent Bible witness to a central and stationary earth.

The culminant effect of the more than 100 Scripture passages based on those of the Creation Week is emphatic; the Bible is a geocentric Book. *Let an attempt be made to present heliocentricity from the Bible! How many passages do you suppose could be presented? I am not aware of a single passage.*

Part III: What History Records

"Flat Earth" Accusation

The claim is made that geocentricity is akin to the old discarded belief in a flat earth. This is a red herring kind of argument designed to divert from the facts of the case. It does not square with the facts. The Bible does not teach a flat earth. There is no historical record that Europe ever believed in a flat earth. There is no history of Christians believing in a flat earth. The ancients saw the roundness of earth in eclipses. As early as 200 BC Erastothenes was able to measure the earth's circumference.

Ptolemy the premier astronomer of the ancient world knew that the earth was spherical.

> He pointed out that people living to the east saw the sun rise earlier, and how much earlier was proportional to how far east they were located. He also noted that, though all must see a lunar eclipse simultaneously, those to the east will see it as later, e.g. at 1 a.m., say, instead of midnight, local time. He also observed that on traveling to the north, Polaris rises in the sky, so this suggests the earth is curved in that direction too. Finally, on approaching a hilly island from far away on a calm sea, he noted that the island seemed to rise out of the sea. He attributed this phenomenon (correctly) to the curvature of the earth. (Michael Fowler, *How the Greeks Used Geometry to Understand the Stars*)

In an attempt to ridicule the Christian faith, two secular writers of the 19th Century, John Draper (1811-1882) and Andrew White (1832-1918) fabricated the flat earth idea. The concept has *no* significant basis in European History. Professor Jeffrey Russell describes this in his 1991 book, *Inventing the Flat Earth: Columbus and Modern History*.

In the following we see that geocentricity was the prevailing, and in fact only view across the centuries.

The Early Jewish View: Geocentric

As the Old Testament is geocentric, it naturally follows that early Jewish writings as the Talmud would also be geocentric. This clearly obvious fact is here stated from *Jewish Encylopedia.com*:

> The Talmud subscribes, as do all astronomers before the time of Copernicus, to the geocentric world conception, according to which the stars move about the earth. ("Ancient Conceptions of Astronomy in the Talmud").

Babylonian Astronomy: Geocentric, With One Exception

As revealed in the *Astronomical Cuneiform Texts*, Babylonian astronmy was highly developed, widely influential, and geocentric. History records only one astronomer from ancient Babylon who was not geocentric.

> Strabo lists Seleucus as one of the four most influential Chaldean/Babylonian astronomers, alongside Kidenas (Kidinnu), Naburianos (Naburimannu) and Sudines. …Seleucus, however, was unique among them in that he was the only one known to have supported the heliocentric theory of planetary motion proposed by Aristarchus. ("Seleucus of Seleucia, c. 190 BC ?" The SAO/NASA Astrophysics Data System - ADS).

Greek Astronomy: Geocentric, With One Exception

All of the known Greek Astronomers were geocentric; the sole execption was Aristarchus of Samos (310-230 BC).

> He was the first person to present an explicit argument for a heliocentric model of the solar system, placing the Sun, not the Earth, at the center of the known universe. He was influenced by the Pythagorean Philolaus of Croton, but, in contrast to Philolaus, he had both identified the central fire with the Sun, as well as putting other planets in correct order from the Sun. (*Wickipedia*).

In c.130 BC, the astronomer Hipparchus presented a detailed refutation of Aristarchus' theory. Nothing further is recorded on behalf of heliocentricity until Nicolas Copernicus took up Aristarchus' views in the Sixteenth Century.

It is a stark fact that *only two* named astronomers from the ancient world are known to have been heliocentric.

> The only other astronomer from antiquity who is known by name and who is known to have supported Aristarchus' heliocentric model was Seleucus of Seleucia, a Mesopotamian astronomer who lived a century after Aristarchus. (Thomas Heath, *The Copernicus of Antiquity: Aristarchus of Samos* , p. 41).

Further, with only four exceptions, all known geocentric astronomers before Copernicus believed that the earth was stationary. The four geocentricists who said the earth turned on its axis were: Hicetas and Ecphantus of the 5th century BC, and Heraclides Ponticus in the 4th century BC. During the Middle Ages, Jean Buridan (1295-1358) sought to revive this idea.

With this total dominance of geocentricity before Copernicus we now mention the variations within this framework among a number of key astronomers.

Aristotle: Geocentricity with Circular Orbits

The famed Greek philosopher Aristotle (384-322 BC) proposed a geocentric universe composed of circular orbits in 55 crystalline spheres to which the celestial bodies were attached and which rotated at different velocities.

By adjusting the velocities of these concentric spheres, many features of planetary motion could be explained. However, it could not account for the observed retrograde (back and forth) motion of several of the planets.

Hipparchus: Geocentricity with Circular Orbits and Epicycles

When ancient astronomers viewed the sky, they saw the Sun, Moon, and stars moving overhead in a regular fashion. They also saw the "wanderers" or planets. The regularity in the motions of the wandering planets suggested that their positions might be predictable. Though suggested before, (Apollonius of Perga, early 2nd Century BC), Hipparchus (c.190-c.120) developed further the theory of epicycles which was to be at the heart of Ptolemy's planetary system.

The following gives an idea of Hipparchus' overall accomplishments and influence:

> He is known to have been a working astronomer at least from 147 to 127 BC. Hipparchus is considered the greatest ancient astronomical observer and, by some, the greatest overall astronomer of antiquity. He was the first whose quantitative and accurate models for the motion of the Sun and Moon survive. For this he certainly made use of the observations and perhaps the mathematical techniques accumulated over centuries by the Chaldeans from Babylonia. He developed trigonometry and constructed trigonometric tables…With his solar and lunar theories and his trigonometry, he may have been the first to develop a reliable method to predict solar eclipses. (*Wikipedia*, emphasis mine).

Notice the statement about his "quantitative and accurate models for the motion of the Sun". Observation and mathmatical observation convinced nearly every early astronomer that the sun orbited the stationary earth.

Ptolemy: Geocentricity with Circular Orbits, Epicycles and Equants

The famed astronomer Ptolemy, a Grecian, did much of his work at Alexandria during the years AD 127-141. His book, *The Almagest*, became the standard text on astronomy for fifteen centuries until Copernicus and Tycho Brahe.

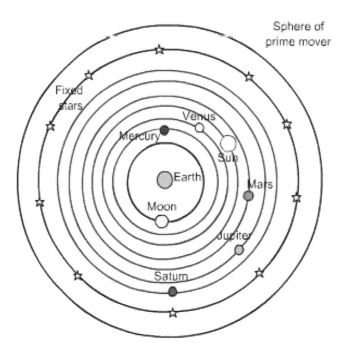

In order to explain the retrograde movement of the planets Ptolemy developed further Hipparchus' theory of epicycles. That is, as the planets circle the earth, they go in a small circle (an epicycle) along their main orbital path. The orbital path is called the "deferent".

Ptolemy proposed that the center of the planet's orbit was not actually on the earth, but at a point somewhat offset. Later, Tycho Brahe, would center the planetary orbits on the sun, and then with the sun and entire solar system circling the earth.

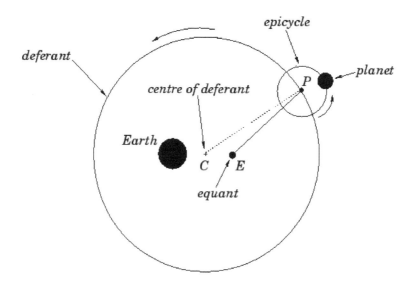

Ptolemy's Planetary System: An Epicycle and Equant For Each Planet

In addition to the earth, and offset center of planetary orbit (center of the deferent), it was necessary for Ptolemy to propose a third point of central reference called the "equant". Without this his system could not adjust to a number of other aspects of planetary motion. For example, the size of a planet's retrograde loop (most notably that of Mars) would be smaller, and sometimes larger. Also the planets were observed to move more rapidly as they were seen closer to the sun.

The *Columbia Encyclopedia* explains:

> Partly on aesthetic grounds and partly because no other hypothesis suggested itself, Ptolemy generally retained the semi-mystical Pythagorean belief that nothing but motion at constant speed in a perfect circle is worthy of a celestial body. He combined simple circular motions to explain the complicated wanderings of the planets against the background of the fixed stars. Ptolemy explained retrograde motion by assuming that each planet moved in a circle called an epicycle, whose center was in turn carried around the earth in a circular orbit called a deferent…The fact that the interior planets (Venus and Mercury) never stray far from the sun was explained by the provision that the centers of their epicycles always had to lie on the line connecting the earth and sun.
>
> In the final version of his system Ptolemy modified the postulate of uniform motion in order to explain the variations in the apparent speeds of the planets. He found that these variations could be reproduced most conveniently by displacing the earth from the center of the deferent to a point called the eccentric. He then assumed that the motion of the center of the epicycle along the deferent appeared uniform, not from the center of the deferent or from the eccentric, but from a third point symmetrically displaced from the eccentric, called the equant. (The Fundamentals of the Ptolemaic System, *Infoplease.com*).

Below are some animations showing how this would work:

http://www.youtube.com/watch?v=FHSWVLwbbNw
http://www.jimloy.com/cindy/ptolemy.htm
http://www.keplersdiscovery.com/Equant.html
http://people.sc.fsu.edu/~dduke/models

The resultant system which eventually came to be widely accepted in the west was an unwieldy one to modern eyes; each planet required an epicycle revolving on a deferent, offset by an equant which was different for each planet. But it predicted various celestial motions, including the beginnings and ends of retrograde motion, fairly well at the time it was developed. (Drawn from *Wikipedia*).

"Epicycles upon Epicycles"

It is claimed that over the course of time more and more epicycles had to be added to Ptolemy's system in order to make it conform to observation. This led to the expression "epicycles upon epicycles" and was said to be a main impetus for the "greatly simplified" heliocentric system of Copernicus – "80 epicycles for Ptolemy, versus a mere 34 for Copernicus". (Robert Palter, *An Approach to the History of Early Astronomy*).

This claim appears to be false and without historical basis:

> According to a school of thought in the history of astronomy, minor imperfections in the original Ptolemaic system were discovered through observations accumulated over time. More levels of epicycles (circles within circles) were added to the models, to match more accurately the observed planetary motions. The multiplication of epicycles is believed to have led to a nearly unworkable system by the 16th century. Copernicus created his heliocentric system in order to simplify the Ptolemaic astronomy of his day, and he succeeded in drastically reducing the number of circles.
>
> A major difficulty with the epicycles-on-epicycles theory is that historians examining books on Ptolemaic astronomy from the Middle Ages and the Renaissance have found no trace of multiple epicycles being used for each planet. The Alfonsine Tables [an alleged source for the epicycles-on-epicycles claim], were apparently computed using Ptolemy's original unadorned methods.
>
> Another problem is that the models themselves discouraged tinkering. In a deferent/epicycle model, the parts of the whole are interrelated. A change in a parameter to improve the fit in one place would throw off the fit somewhere else. Ptolemy's model is probably optimal in this regard. On the whole it gave good results but missed a little here and there. Experienced astronomers would have recognized these shortcomings and allowed for them. (Epicycles upon Epicycles, *Wikipedia*).

In the 1400 years from Ptolemy to Copernicus there are no named or known astronomers who were heliocentricists. There were a number, particularly among Arabic astronomers, who departed from Ptolemy in a number of areas, but nevertheless remained firmly geocentric. Notable among these was Ibn al-Shatir (1304-1375). Some of the computations in his work, *The Final Quest Concerning the Rectification of Principles*, where adapted by Copernicus for his heliocentric model.

Copernicus: Heliocentricity with Circular Orbits and Epicycles – <u>No Proof</u>

We say again: If history has consistently used the word "revolution" to describe an event, there is every likelihood that that is exactly what it is - an event of epic proportion, *A Revolution*. And more so if there is not any geographic (French, Russian) or other limitation given to the event. The fire Copernicus lit was called a "Revolution". It was a revolution in the fullest sense of the word. It completely reshaped the way men thought about the world and of life itself. Only something on this scale could have prepared the way for Darwin. But again: Not even evolution with its universal acceptance has been able to claim the status of a "revolution".

> The dethronement of the Earth from the centre of the universe caused profound shock. No longer could the Earth be considered the epitome of creation...The successful challenge to the entire system of ancient authority required a complete change in man's philosophical

conception of the universe. This is rightly called the "Copernican Revolution". (*Encyclopaedia Britannica*, Vol. 5, p.146)

The "Copernican Revolution" upon which modern "everything" rests is a revolution against the authority of the Bible....The debate was, and still is, over the Bible. The bottom line: either man's science is right or the Bible is right. (James Hanson, *The Bible and Geocentricity*, p. 14)

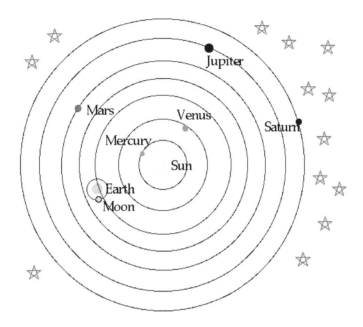

Copernicus' Heliocentric Model

What prompted this fundamental shift? Was it merely dissatisfaction with the complexities of the Ptolemaic system? If so then why not seek to refine it as Tycho Brahe had done? Certainly Copernicus could not fault the basic predictive accuracy of Ptolemy. For 1400 years it served its purpose very well. The answer at least initially seems to have been more philosophic than scientific. Copernicus was influenced by the 2nd Century BC heliocentricity of Aristarchus, but before that, though a staunch Catholic, he imbided Plato's *Republic* in which Plato refers to the sun as the source of all good, even above the "gods".

> "...which of the gods in heaven can you put down as the cause of and master of this, whose light makes our sight see so beautifully and the things to be seen?" "...it is plain that you mean the sun!" (B. Nelson, "The Early Modern Revolution in Science and Philosophy," *Boston Studies in the Philosophy of Science*, 3, p.12).

Notice the near deification Copernicus gives to the sun in the introduction of his *De revolutionibus orbium coelestium*:

In this most beautiful temple of God how could the sun be given a better place to illuminate the whole all at once? Rightly he is called the Lamp, Soul and Ruler of the Universe. Hermes Trismegistus calls him the Visible God while Sophocles's Electra calls him the All-seeing One. Let us place it upon a royal throne, let it truly guide the circling family of planets, earth included. Such a picture—so simple, clear and beautiful. (Book 1, chapter 10, folio 9v. Emphasis mine).

Had Copernicus spent more time in Genesis One than with Plato, he would have understood the secondary nature of the Sun's creation in relation to the earth. He would have seen the significance of Earth being created on the First Day and the Sun not until the Fourth. He could not have missed the simple fact that no statement at all is given to the earth's movement before or after the creation of the Sun - not in Genesis One, not anywhere else in the Bible. Had Copernicus gone to the Scriptures he would have seen much that pointed in the opposite direction - a stationary earth.

There is the common misconception that Copernicus' system did not need to use epicycles: The following overview of the two systems shows this to be false:

When Copernicus transformed Earth-based observations to heliocentric coordinates, he was confronted with an entirely new problem. The Sun-centered positions displayed a cyclical motion with respect to time but without retrograde loops in the case of the outer planets. In principle, the heliocentric motion was simpler but with new subtleties due to the yet-to-be-discovered elliptical shape of the orbits. Another complication was caused by a problem that Copernicus never solved: correctly accounting for the motion of the Earth in the coordinate transformation. In keeping with past practice, Copernicus used the deferent/epicycle model in his theory but his epicycles were small and were called "epicyclets". (Owen Gingerich, *The Book Nobody Read*, p. 267).

In the Ptolemaic system the models for each of the planets were different and so it was with Copernicus' initial models. As he worked through the mathematics, however, Copernicus discovered that his models could be combined in a unified system. Furthermore, if they were scaled so that Earth's orbit was the same in all of them, the ordering of the planets we recognize today literally fell out of the math. Mercury orbited closest to the Sun and the rest of the planets fell into place in order outward, arranged in distance by their periods of revolution. (Gingerich, p. 267).

Whether or not Copernicus' models were simpler than Ptolemy's is moot. Copernicus eliminated Ptolemy's somewhat-maligned equant but at a cost of additional epicycles. Various 16th-century books based on Ptolemy and Copernicus use about equal numbers of epicycles. The idea that Copernicus used only 34 circles in his system comes from his own statement in a preliminary unpublished sketch called the *Commentariolus*. By the time he published *De revolutionibus orbium coelestium*, he had added more circles. Counting the total number is difficult, but estimates are that he created a system just as complicated, or even more so ….Copernicus' work provided explanations for phenomena like retrograde motion, but really didn't prove that the planets actually orbited the Sun. (Gingerich, *Alfonso X as a Patron of Astronomy*, in *The Eye of Heaven: Ptolemy, Copernicus, Kepler* p. 125, emphasis mine).

One writer goes further in the number of epicycles Copernicus needed for his system:

> The popular belief that Copernicus' heliocentric system constitutes a significant simplification of the Ptolemaic system is obviously wrong....the Copernican models themselves require about twice as many circles as the Ptolemaic models and are far less elegant and adaptable. (O. Neugebauer, *The Exact Sciences in Antiquity*, p. 204).

Despite these problems and the lack real empirical evidence to justify such the change, a fire was lit, a revolution begun; but on the day Copernicus received his copy of *De revolutionibus orbium coelestium* from the publisher - he died - May 24, 1543.

Tycho Brahe: Geocentricity with the Sun Orbiting the Earth and the Planet's Orbiting the Sun

Today the names Copernicus, Kepler, Galileo, and Newton are far better known than Tycho Brahe (1546-1601). In the16th Century, however, the premier figure in European astronomy was the Danish geocentricist Tycho Brahe. Tycho (called by first name in Denmark and Scandinavian countries) is credited with the most accurate astronomical observations up to his time. No one before had attempted to make so many planetary observations. He was to be the last major astronomer to work without the aid of a telescope. Yet as the following shows the scale of his work as evidenced by the size of his intrumentents was astounding.

Tycho's Extraordinary Instruments

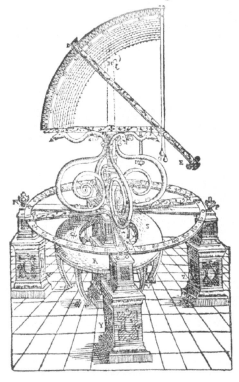

The Brass Azimuthal Quadrant 1576

The Computational Globe 1580

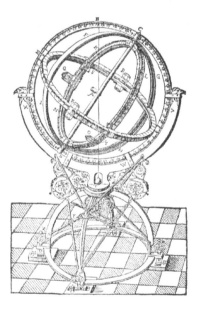

The Armillary Sphere 1581

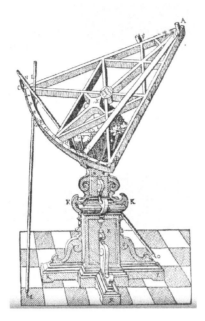

Triangular Sextant 1582

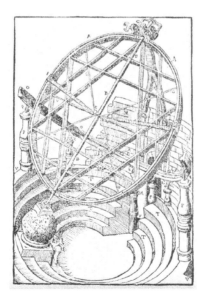

Great Equatorial Armillary 1585

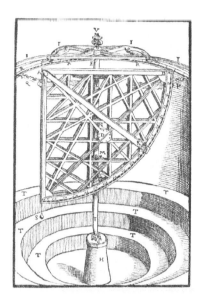

Revolving Quadrant 1586

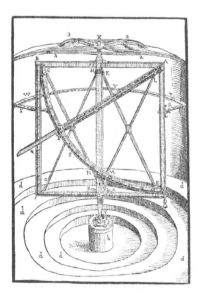

Revolving Steel Quadrant 1588

The Great Quadrant of Uraniborg 1852

These magnificent instruments constructed by numerous craftsmen and financed by the Danish government were at that time far beyond anything the world had seen. They were a monument to Tycho's prodigious labours, and help explain the acclaimed accuracy of his calculations. The following gives a brief account:

> King Frederick II (ruled 1559–1588) offered him lordship over the island of Hveen, where, in the summer of 1576, he laid the foundation stone for his new manor house which he named Uraniborg—castle of the heavens….Each end of the second floor of the building housed an array of instruments located under removable roof sections. Tycho had ordered the first of his permanent instruments for measuring angles between celestial objects while in Augsburg and he added to his collection at Uraniborg, continuing to expand the sizes, designs, and materials of these instruments, building a special workshop nearby and employing trained craftsmen for this purpose.

> Finding that subtle movements of the instruments caused by the wind or by unsteady supports limited the accuracy of observations, Tycho built Stjærneborg ('castle of the stars'), an observatory comprising a central room surrounded by five pits dug into the ground, each of which was covered by a removable lid and housed a particular instrument that was set upon a stone foundation to reduce vibration. With large instruments of such quality, he attained unprecedented accuracy. Christian IV, however, succeeded Frederick II, assuming the throne in 1596, and began to cut Tycho's funding. In response, Tycho packed up his instruments and left Denmark in 1597, securing a position as imperial astronomer to the Holy Roman emperor Rudolf II, who provided him a castle near Prague in which to re-establish his research facilities, both astronomical and alchemical. At this point Tycho hired Johannes Kepler to assist him with the calculations necessary to

establish a new astronomical theory on the basis of his accurate data. ("Tycho Brahe," *Encyclopedia. com*).

Sadly the use of these great instruments was to end with Tycho's death in 1601.

> After his death, legal battles between Kepler and Tycho's heirs led to the instruments being stored away. All but Tycho's great globe were destroyed in the aftermath of the Bohemian civil war of 1619. The great globe found its way back to Copenhagen, and remained in the University's observatory tower until that tower and all its content were destroyed by fire in 1728. All we know about Tycho's instruments is from his published writings. (www.astro.umontreal.ca/~paulchar/sp/images/tycho.3.html).

The Rudolphine Tables

Tycho had intended that his copious star and planetary tables be dedicated to the Holy Roman Emperor Rudolf II, but by the time of their publication in 1627 and their being adapted to heliocentricity by Johannes Keplar; Rudolf had died, and were instead dedicated to Emperor Ferdinand II, but with the original name retained.

The tables contain positions for the 1,006 stars measured by Tycho, and 400 and more stars from Ptolemy and Johann Bayer, and with directions and tables for locating and predicting planetary positions. Most of his data was accurate to within 1/60th of one degree, i.e., to within 1 arc minute.

The Rudolphine Tables

As an example of their accuracy, Tycho's tables predicted two planetary transits (a passing of a planet between the Sun and Earth) nearly forty years after his death.

> The tables were sufficiently accurate to predict a transit of Mercury observed by Pierre Gassendi in 1631 and a transit of Venus observed by Jeremiah Horrox in 1639. (A. Athreya and O. Gingerich, *An Analysis of Kepler's Rudolphine Tables and Implications for the Reception of His Physical Astronomy*).

Tycho's Planetary System

Tycho proposed a system in which the Sun and Moon orbited the Earth, while the planets orbited the Sun.

> His system provided a safe position for astronomers who were dissatisfied with older models but were reluctant to accept the Earth's motion. It gained a considerable following after 1616 when Rome decided officially that the heliocentric model was contrary to both philosophy and Scripture, and could be discussed only as a computational convenience that had no connection to fact. (Victor Thoren, *Tycho Brahe* pp. 14-15).

Both Ptolemy's geocentric model and the heliocentric system of Copernicus relied upon a system of deferents and epicycles. But in Tycho's system with the sun orbiting the earth and the planets orbiting the sun, the sun's orbit in effect becomes the *deferent* and the planet's orbits the *epicycles* – at least in comparison to the previous systems. (See Philip Stott, *The Earth Our Home*, p.14).

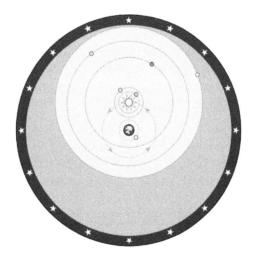

The Tychonic System

In this depiction of the Tychonic system, the objects on blue orbits (the moon and the sun) revolve around the earth. The objects on orange orbits (Mercury, Venus, Mars, Jupiter, and Saturn) revolve around the sun. Around all is sphere of fixed stars. Heraclides in the 4th century BC, and several of Tycho's contemporaries proposed similar systems but with the crucial difference that their's had the earth spinning, while with Tycho the earth is stationary.

Tycho believed that if the Earth orbited the Sun annually there should be an observable stellar parallax (angular movement of the nearer stars against the background stars) over a period of six months. None was detected until 1838 when Friedrich Bessel is said to have discovered a stellar parallax of 0.314 arc-seconds for the star 61 Cygni. This so-called "proof" of earth's motion will be examined later.

Helmer Aslaksen makes several important points concerning Tycho's system:

> **Myth: Galileo's discovery of the entire cycle of phases of Venus was proof of the truth of the Copernican system.** The phases of Venus went against the Ptolemaic system, but not against Tycho Brahe's system….

> **Myth: The battle was between the Copernican and the Ptolemaic systems.** Tycho Brahe introduced his geostatic, heliocentric system in 1588, and it quickly won the support of the Catholic Church. It is very interesting that Galileo does not discuss Tycho's system in his 1632 book. Probably because he realized that it would be very hard for him to argue against it! (*Myths about the Copernican Revolution*).

Tycho's Sudden Death

In apparently good health and at the age of only 54, history's greatest pre-telescope astronomer was taken ill at a banquet in Prague, and died eleven days later, on 24 October 1601. A urinary infection had long been thought to be the cause. Before dying, he urged Kepler to finish the *Rudolphine Tables* and expressed the hope that he would do so by adopting Tycho's own planetary system, rather than Copernicus's. A contemporary physician attributed his death to a kidney stone, but no kidney stones were found during an autopsy performed after his body was exhumed in 1901.

> Recent investigations have suggested that Tycho did not die from urinary problems but instead from mercury poisoning—extremely toxic levels of it have been found in hairs from his moustache. The results were, however, not conclusive. ("Rotten in the State of Denmark", *Der Spiegel*, January 16, 2009).

Tycho's body is interred in a tomb in the Church of Our Lady in Old Town Square near the Prague Astronomical Clock. The Prague City Hall has approved a request by Danish scientists to exhume the remains. A team from Aarhus University began their work in November 2010.

Interest was heightened in 2004 with the publication of the extensively researched
Heavenly Intrigue: Johannes Kepler, Tycho Brahe, and the Murder Behind One of History's Greatest Scientific Discoveries, (Doubleday). The authors Joshua and Ann-Lee Gilder present the astonishing claim that not only was Brahe murdered but that the chief suspect could only have been his resident mathematician *Johannes Kepler.*

That the book is substantial and should not be immediately dismissed can seen by the extent of the original and onsite research gathered by the authors.

Acknowledgement of this is given in a number of reviews:

> Kepler has always ranked as one of the great geniuses of Renaissance science. But two investigative reporters now wish to place him in a very different pantheon: that of a brilliant Renaissance criminal. Interpreting astonishing new forensic evidence in the light of careful archival research, the Gilders allege that Kepler used his powerful mind to plot the perfect murder, secretly poisoning his employer--the astronomer Tycho Brahe--to secure astronomical data he needed to advance his own pioneering work. The authors recount a familiar story in chronicling the improbable events that gave the audacious Kepler his post as a disgruntled assistant to the flamboyant but conceptually cautious Brahe. However, the Gilders depart dramatically from the long-standard history in explaining the death of the Danish astronomer. In new X-ray emission studies of Brahe's remains, the Gilders find proof that the astronomer died of mercury poisoning--not from natural causes, as previously assumed. Through some sharp-eyed sleuthing, the authors then build a strong circumstantial case against Kepler as the cunning culprit. Their remarkable detective work will win praise from mystery buffs and historians alike. Bryce Christensen, (*American Library Association*).

> The authors present cutting-edge forensic evidence of mercury poison in Brahe's remains. To further build their case, they offer transcripts of letters and papers never before translated from Latin and interpretations from historians of astronomy. ... The story is carefully documented and the science behind the men's work is clearly laid out. (*Science News*).

> ... the Gilders have produced a brilliant, readable, and original historical work that ought to convince readers that one of history's greatest scientist committed a cold-blooded murder. (*National Review*).

Further summary of the Gilders findings is seen in the following:

> Despite his genius, Kepler was by some accounts a difficult person to like: vindictive, jealous, and prone to violent rages when he didn't get his way. There is little doubt that he appropriated the data of his mentor, Tycho Brahe, and used it for his own purposes; Kepler openly admitted as much, and evidently felt not the slightest pang of conscience. But recent forensic evidence hints that Kepler may have done more than steal from Brahe — he might have murdered him as well....

> Despite Brahe's saintly patience and willingness to secure a salary and lodgings for Kepler, the younger astronomer often stormed out of the house or wrote letters to friends insulting Brahe and his family. A few surviving letters also confirm that Kepler was trying to manipulate acquaintances into helping him secure Brahe's data, which he felt he needed in order to prove his own theories.

> At fifty-four, Brahe had always been a healthy person. But on October 13, 1601, Brahe was attending a banquet when he suddenly fell ill, delirious and unable to urinate. Over the next

eleven days, the astronomer hovered at the point of death, suffering from fever and severe abdominal pain.

On the evening of October 23, he seemed to rally somewhat; his fever broke, his pain subsided, and he regained lucidity. But by the next morning he was dead. Until recently, it was thought that Brahe had died from uremia, or possibly from a burst bladder. But recent forensic analysis of his hair shows a curious spike in the amount of mercury in Brahe's body shortly before his death….

The amount of mercury in Brahe's hair sample, analyzed in the early 1990s, was enormous, and actually suggested two separate poisonings: The first at the dinner party, where he had suddenly fallen ill, and the second the night before his death, when his condition had seemed to be improving. A spike in his calcium level a few hours before his death suggests that the poison was administered in a glass of milk.

Although there are many other possible explanations for Brahe's death, not all of them involving murder, Joshua and Ann-Lee Gilder, in their book *Heavenly Intrigue*, argue that Kepler was the most likely suspect. Kepler was well versed in alchemy and had access to Brahe's alchemical lab, and he had often expressed his hatred of Brahe in letters; he felt that merely being Brahe's assistant would never bring him any glory.

There was also the case of the data, which Kepler made no secret of wanting to get his hands on; indeed, after Brahe's death, even though the older astronomer had asked for the logbooks to go to his family, Kepler took off with them. Brahe's son-in-law was able to wrest most of the books back from Kepler's grasp, but only after Kepler had copied all the data he needed out of them. (Jenny Ashford, *Did Johannes Kepler Murder Tycho Brahe?*).

Johannes Kepler did much to bring an end to the common belief in geocentricity. Whether he brought an end to Tycho Brahe is a matter over which the evidence may never be more than circumstantial. The current exhumation may give further clues.

There is no doubt, however, concerning the boiling resentment Kepler felt toward his mentor as the chief obstruction toward his own goals, and of refusing him unfettered access to his observations.

One of the striking things about Kelper's attitude toward Brahe is how quickly it hardened into bitter hostility. Brahe, he complained to Mastlin after he received that first letter….he was thinking of "striking Tycho himself with a sword". (*Heavenly Intrigue*, p. 242).

Tycho's Body Exhumed

News of the exhumation was relayed by major news agencies on November 15, 2010. The following is from Reuters.

PRAGUE | Mon Nov 15, 2010 12:24pm EST
PRAGUE(Reuters Life!) - Was it accidental poison or murder most foul? Could it

have been a sudden illness or the dark result of envy among two of history's greatest astronomers?

Czech and Danish scientists opened the Prague tomb of Danish astronomer Tycho Brahe on Monday in an attempt to discover what killed the alchemist in 1601, whose observations of celestial bodies laid the foundations for modern astronomy and his assistant Johannes Kepler's later fame.

Speculation has long centered around three theories. Brahe -- who worked at the Prague court of Holy Roman Emperor Rudolph II and is a popular figure in Czech and Danish history -- was murdered, became ill or simply ingested too much of a toxic substance such as mercury in the course of his experiments.

The Czech Academy of Sciences said nuclear scientists will test bone and hair samples taken from Brahe's remains in the Our Lady Before Tyn Church in Prague's medieval Old Town Square.

They will be looking for mercury and other substances that could shed light on the cause of his death. Some presence of mercury was shown by earlier analysis of his facial hair. Scientists said longer-term exposure to poison would indicate Brahe may have died from self-administered "medicine" or too much exposure from his experiments. However, high concentrations of a toxic substance near the hair root could indicate a big one-time dose of poison. "Generally the finding of high concentrations of a toxic element, such as arsenic, in sequential hair samples of a potential murder victim is considered an indicator of a murder and can be used as evidence," said Jan Kucera from the Nuclear Physics Institute in Rez near Prague.

One murder theory says that Brahe was killed on the orders of Danish King Christian IV who he had fallen out with or that his now more famous assistant Johannes Kepler murdered him to get his hands on Brahe's astronomic observations. An illness causing kidney failure is another possibility…

Further tests will be done at universities in Lund, Sweden and Odense, Denmark, the Czech Academy of Sciences said.

A preliminary report in *The Guardian* released 15 November 2012 ruled out death by mercury poisoning.

Ever since Tycho Brahe died suddenly more than 400 years ago, there has been mystery about whether the Dane whose observations laid the groundwork for modern astronomy fell victim to natural causes or was murdered.

On Thursday, scientists who had exhumed his body said one thing was clear: if he was murdered, it wasn't with mercury, as many rumours had claimed.

"We measured the concentration of mercury using three different quantitative chemical methods in our labs," said Kaare Lund Rasmussen, associate professor of chemistry at the

University of Southern Denmark. "All tests revealed the same result: that mercury concentrations were not sufficiently high to have caused his death. In fact, chemical analyses of the bones indicate that Tycho Brahe was not exposed to an abnormally high mercury load in the last five to 10 years of his life," Rasmussen said in a statement. The scientists did not say what did kill the astronomer, but tests on the remains are still being conducted.

Brahe's death in 1601 at the age of 54 was long believed to have been due to a bladder infection…But some speculated that he might have been poisoned with mercury even at the hands of a king or a rival astronomer.

"Brahe's famous assistant [astronomer] Johannes Kepler has been identified as a possible murder suspect, and other candidates have been singled out for suspicion throughout the years," said Jens Vellev, a professor of medieval archaeology at Aarhus University, Denmark, who heads the Czech-Danish team of scientists that conducted the research…

Tests conducted in 1996 in Sweden, and later in Denmark, on samples of Brahe's moustache and hair obtained in a 1901 exhumation showed unusually high levels of mercury, supporting the poisoning theory. But Vellev was unsatisfied with that conclusion and he won permission from the church and Prague authorities to reopen the tomb, saying the remains needed to be analysed with contemporary technology.

His team opened Brahe's tomb in the Church of Our Lady Before Tyn near Prague's Old Town Square two years ago. Tests on Brahe's beard and bones resolved the mercury question, Vellev said, but work is still being done on his teeth and that could determine his cause of death. (guardian.co.uk, 15 November 2012).

Tychonic Astronomy after Tycho

Galileo's 1610 telescopic discovery that Venus shows a full set of phases similar to the moon provided an argument against the Ptolemaic model. As a result much of 17th century astronomy moved to geo-heliocentric planetary models like Tycho's that could explain these phases just as well as Copernicus' heliocentric model, but without the latter's disadvantage of failure to detect any annual stellar parallax.

In 1622 Tycho's assistant and disciple, Christen Longomontanus, published *Astronomia Danica*. This with Tycho's observational data was intended to be the full statement of his master's planetary model. However, it became known as "the semi-Tychonic" version, for Longomontanus contradicted his master and proposed a daily rotating Earth.

What *may* have caused this change is here explained:

> A conversion of astronomers to geo-rotational geo-heliocentric models with a daily rotating Earth such as that of Longomontanus <u>may</u> have been precipitated by Francesco Sizzi's 1613 discovery of annually periodic seasonal variations of sunspot trajectories across the sun's disc. They appear to oscillate above and below its apparent equator over the course

of the four seasons. This seasonal variation is explained much better by the hypothesis of a daily rotating Earth together with that of the sun's axis being tilted throughout its supposed annual orbit than by that of a daily orbiting sun, if not even refuting the latter hypothesis because it predicts a daily vertical oscillation of a sunspot's position, contrary to observation. This discovery and its import for heliocentrism, but not for geo-heliocentrism, is discussed in the Third Day of Galileo's 1632 *Dialogo*. (See p. 345-56 of Stillman Drake's 1967 *Dialogue concerning the two chief world systems*. But see Drake's *Sunspots, Sizzi and Scheiner'* in his 1970 *Galileo Studies* for its critical discussion of Galileo's misleading presentation of this phenomenon. Emphasis mine).

The extended footnote points to a problem with Sizzi's discovery being used as evidence for heliocentricity. See below on *Galileo's "Proofs" for Heliocentricity*.

The further demise of Tychonic astronomy is described in the following:

> The fact that Longomontanus's book was republished in two later editions in 1640 and 1663 no doubt reflected the popularity of Tychonic astronomy in the 17th century. Its adherents included John Donne and the atomist and astronomer Pierre Gassendi. The ardent anti-heliocentric French astronomer Jean-Baptiste Morin devised a Tychonic planetary model with elliptical orbits published in 1650 in a simplified, Tychonic version of the *Rudolphine Tables*, (René Taton, Curtis Wilson, *Planetary astronomy from the Renaissance to the rise of astrophysics Part A*, pp. 42, 50, 166).

> Some acceptance of the Tychonic system persisted through the 17th century and in places until the early 18th century; it was supported (after a 1633 decree about the Copernican controversy) by "a flood of pro-Tycho literature" of Jesuit origin. Among pro-Tycho Jesuits, Ignace Pardies declared in 1691 that it was still the commonly accepted system, and Francesco Blanchinus reiterated that as late as 1728….But in Germany, Holland, and England, the Tychonic system "vanished from the literature much earlier".(Christine Schofield, *The Tychonic and Semi-Tychonic World Systems*, pp. 41,43).

Geocentricists today generally hold to the Tychonian system, and Tycho's view of the stationary earth in the centre. A notable exception is Professor James Hanson. In his *The Bible and Geocentricity* he says:

> I do not subscribe to the Tychonic model for I do not find it in Scripture; however, I do find strict geocentricity whereby the earth is the center of all celestial motions. Parallax and aberration (and other optical-angular effects such as possible light bending near massive bodies) can be explained within the strict geocentric model….I have spent considerable time developing such a strictly geocentric model. This model regards the earth as a vortex-sink…..pp. 86,87.

With the death of Tycho Brahe in 1601, scientific support for the geocentric world view began to decline rapidly. But at that time another event was taking place: the preparation of the King James Bible! When truth fades in one area it persists in another. The AV in contrast to modern bibles is a Geocentric Bible. Truth will always have a first and continuing voice.

The Neo-Tychonic Model: Geocentricity with Planets in Elliptical Orbit Around the Sun

Tycho centered the planets on the sun, but the stars were centered on the earth. This system later was found not to allow for the phenomena known as stellar parallax: the apparent movement of nearer stars against background stars over a six-month period. Stellar parallax was not observed until 1838. The Tyconic model favored by many geocentrists today, and which can account for parallax, centers the the stars on the sun. This slight adjustment places the stationary earth, if not exactly, *nearly so* at the center of the cosmos.

In addition as Kepler's laws of planetary motion were to a large extent based on Tycho's observational data, an eliptical rather than circular planetary orbit is generally favored in the Neo-Tyconic model.

Therefore Scripture (which requires a stationary earth, but not necessarily its absolute centrality) and observation (which detects parallax) are both satisfied. Further, the Neo-Tyconic model can accommodate both a large or small uninverse, whereas Tycho's original version (chiefly because of parallax) was only adaptable to a small universe. (See Robert Sungenis, *Galileo Was Wrong, The Church Was Right*, pp. 348,349).

Johannes Kepler: Heliocentricity with Earth and Planets Elliptically Orbiting the Sun – <u>No Proof</u>

Tycho carefully guarded his large body of celestial measurements, *and* Johannes Kepler admitted that he "usurped" them following Tycho's death. See, Stephen Hawking, *On the Shoulders of Giant*, p. 108).

As we move now to Johannes Kepler, we come to a man who brings new meaning to the word "enigma". In a book for younger readers, John H. Tiner in his *Giant of Faith and Science Johannes Keplar* presents Kepler in a typically positive light, and especially in comparison with the bombastic Tycho Brahe. Kepler is ever the faithful Christian and Tycho's longsuffering mathematician being forced to provide formulae for an astronomical system he does not accept. He is blocked from realising his own pursuits – the completion of his *Cosmic Mystery* – and is refused full access to Tycho's observations.

Other researchers (a minority) do not share this assessment:

> Brahe was a fervent empirical thinker who devoted his life to mapping the heavens, Kepler, too neasighted to make his own observations was an endless font of theory and speculation, much of it highly mystical and misguided, some of it breathtakingly brilliant.

> But Kepler's brilliant mind had a dark side that was tormented by rage, fear, and jealousy – and obsessed wth the desire to possess Tycho Brahe's massive store of planeraty observations as his own. (Joshua Gilder, Anne-Lee Gilder, *Heavenly Intrigue*, p. 3).

Against the backdrop of this "dark side", the passage from the Sixteenth to the Seventeenth Century would be critical for geocentricity. Kepler ultimately published the *Rudolphine Tables* containing the star catalog and planetary tables using Tycho's measurements. This however was not until 1627. He had been hard-pressed to fight off Tycho's numerous relatives. They argued that Tycho's work should benefit his own family, and not one of Tycho's competitors. Kepler counter argued that he and Tycho had been collaborating on the data for many years before Tycho's death and asserted that he was responsible for most of the calculations and also for the organization of the data.

In the end Kepler did win control of the tables and published them without the Brahe family receiving any monetary benefit. Brahe had intended that the tables should be dedicated to Emperor Rudolf II, but by 1627 he had died, and they were instead dedicated to Emperor Ferdinand II while retaining the name *Rudolphine Tables*.

Kepler's model of elliptical orbits around the sun was to be a refinement of Copernicus' model which was based on perfect circles and epicycles.

Kepler's Three Laws of Planetary Motion

In *adapting* Tycho's data to heliocentricity, Kepler published his three laws of planetary motion. His first two were published in 1609 and the third in 1619. The key word here is *adaptation*. Tycho's geocentric planetary system reflected very well the vast store of observational data he had gathered. For Kepler to make the data fit heliocentricity would require fundamental change. After a great deal of trial and error the change that seemed to make the data work for a sun centred system was the use of elliptical rather then circular planetary orbits. Such a theory with its constantly changing planetary velocity was a quantum leap in the history of astronomy.

The following gives a brief summary of these laws.

1. The Law of Ellipses: The orbits of the planets are ellipses, with the Sun as one of the two foci.

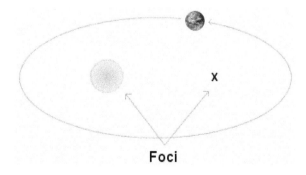

The Law of Ellipses states that the orbit of each planet is an ellipse having two foci, with the center of the sun being at one focus. There is no physical significance of the second non-sun focus but it does have mathematical significance. The total distance from a planet to each of the foci added together is always the same regardless of where the planet is in its orbit.

Kepler's Law of Ellipses requires that the orbital speed of a planet around the sun is constantly increasing or decreasing throughout the planet's "year." It increases when the planet is approaching and nearest the sun (called the *perihelion*), and is at its slowest when it is farthest away (*aphelion*).

In one sense a circle is also an ellipse – an ellipse with 0 eccentricity, and in which the foci coincide in the center of the circle. Most planets have orbits that are far more nearly circular than the diagrams suggest. But they are not circles, but rather ellipses with non-zero eccentricity.

2. The Law of Equal Areas in Equal Times: The line joining a planet to the Sun sweeps out equal areas in equal times as the planet travels around the ellipse.

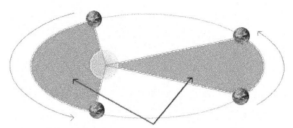

Sweeping out equal area in equal time

The Law of Equal Areas in Equal Times describes the speed at which a planet will move while orbiting the sun. In any given amount of time, 80 days for instance, the planet sweeps out the same amount of area regardless of which 80-day period you choose. The amount of the area remains the same despite the differences of the "shape of the sweep". The areas formed when the earth is closest to the sun can be approximated as a wide but short triangle; whereas the areas formed when the earth is farthest from the sun can be shown as a narrow but long triangle. These areas are the same size. Since the *base* of these triangles are longer when the earth is furthest from the sun, the earth would have to be moving more slowly in order for this imaginary area to be the same size as when the earth is closest to the sun.

An essential unit of measure in Kepler's third law is the *semi-major axis*, which by utilizing the second foci gives in the ellipse the average distance of the planet to the sun (i.e. as contrasted with variable radius of the planet to the sun).

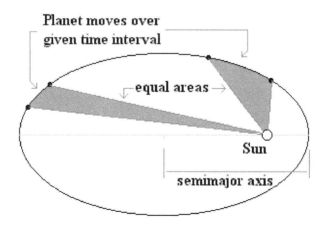

**3. The Law of Harmonies: The square of the total time period (T) of the orbit is proportional to the cube of the average distance of the planet to the Sun (R). **

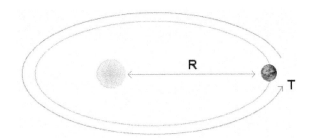

The Law of Harmonies compares the orbital time period and average radius (semi-major axis) of an orbit of any planet to those of the other planets. The discovery Kepler made is that the *ratio* of the square of the orbital time period to the cube of the semi-major axis is the same (or nearly so) for every planet. Hence this third law has been called the Law of Harmonies.

Therefore if you know the period or time of a planet's orbit (T), then you can determine that planet's distance from the Sun (a = the semi-major axis of the planet's orbit) and *vice versa*. This is because the ratios between the two are always the same. The ratio is T^2/a^3, or also expressed as T^2/R^3.

Kepler's formula shows, for example, that those planets far from the sun with longer periods have the same ratio or proportion between the square of the period and the cube of the semi-major axis as those nearer the sun. Thus from this Kepler was able to calculate planetary distance. (Adapted from *Western Washington University Planetarium*, *Physics Classroom*, **Platonic Realms Interactive Encylopedia**).

As shown in the following chart (from *Physics Classroom*) Kepler's laws became the basis for current figures of planetary distances in the heliocentric system. As the earth to sun distance was considered to be much less in his day than in modern times, these figures will differ from what Kepler calculated, but the basis of calculation remains the same. Here the *Period* for each planet is given in earth years, and the Average Distance or *au* of the planet's distance from the sun is given in *astronomical units* (the distance of the earth from the sun). Note again that the T^2/R^3 ratio is nearly the same for all the planets. This is acknowledged to be an *amazing* fact!

Planet	Period (yr)	Ave. Dist. (au)	T^2/R^3 (yr^2/au^3)
Mercury	*0.241*	*0.39*	*0.98*
Venus	*.615*	*0.72*	*1.01*
Earth	*1.00*	*1.00*	*1.00*
Mars	*1.88*	*1.52*	*1.01*
Jupiter	*11.8*	*5.20*	*0.99*
Saturn	*29.5*	*9.54*	*1.00*
Uranus	*84.0*	*19.18*	*1.00*
Neptune	*165*	*30.06*	*1.00*
Pluto	*248*	*39.44*	*1.00*

Except for the fact that the earth is stationary and at the center, and that circular rather than elliptical orbits were envisaged by Tyco, these figures would apparently be nearly that which is required by the Tychonic system.

It is important to remember that it was Tycho's data, and specifically his observational data on Mars that provided the basis of his Third Law and T^2/R^3 ratio.

> In the case of Mars, Kepler used data from Tyco Brahe to figure out the orbital period and distance of this planet -- not the Third Law of Planetary Motion, which had yet to be conceived. Kepler's stroke of genius was to derive his Laws of Planetary Motion from what he knew about Mars -- and then to apply them to the other planets as well. In fact, Kepler's Third Law governs all bodies orbiting the Sun, including asteroids and comets. (idialstars.com).

It has long been an open question among students of the history of astronomy as to the extent that Kepler's laws were based on Tycho's data and to what extent he "launched out on his own."

Kepler's Dream

Despite the acclaimed brilliance of Kepler's laws, a writing called the *Dream* was clearly not a *stroke of genius*. Once the earth is removed from its place at the center of the cosmos, and it becomes but another planet, discordant ideas begin to emerge, including that of extra-terrestrial life. Intertwined with his mother being accused of witchcraft and he himself accused of being an accomplice we have Kepler's strange fictional work about *life on the moon*.

Gilder and Gilder explain:

> Kepler was convinced the blame [the accusation of being an accomplice to his mother's witchcraft] lay in his privately distributed *Somnium*, or "Dream", the short fantasy of travel to the moon, which is written in the first person and full of autobiographical elements. The hero's single mother makes a living selling her witch brews as charms. Angry with her son for spoiling a sale, she sends him off with a captain, who in turn leaves the little boy on Tycho Brahe's island of Hven. There he would learn astronomy. The descriptions of the witch uncomfortably matched his own beleaguered mother, or at least the view most of her neighbors held of the mumbling, cantankerous old woman - a connection underlined in the opening pages, in which the mother, who calls forth spirits in secret ceremonies, personally introduces her son to the demons who will transport him to the moon….
>
> Whatever his motive may have been, he set about revising the *Somnium* in the latter part of the 1620s, adding some fifty pages of detailed footnotes, attempting to explain away what superstitious minds had taken as an allusive but damning indictment of his mother. It was the last major work he would produce.

On Kepler's moon, "a race of serpents predominates." They "have no settled dwellings, no fixed habitation" and "wander in hordes over the whole globe," creeping into caves or diving deep underwater to escape the burning sun, for "whatever clings to the surface is boiled by the sun at midday and becomes food for the approaching swarms of inhabitants."

In the fall of 1630, before the publication of the *Somnium* could be completed, the abandoned boy, now an aging man, would abandon his own family. The reasons for his leaving are not entirely clear, but in his depression and despondency he seems to have known he was heading toward his death. In a note on the yearly horoscope he charted for himself, Kepler had observed that all the planets occupied the same position as at the time of his birth. He carted away all his books and clothes and the written documents "containing all his wealth," leaving his family penniless. (*Heavenly Intrigue*, pp.261,262).

Coming back to Kepler's purpose in writing about this trip to the moon, he could not have been more specific:

> The object of my *Dream*, was to work out, through the example of the moon, an argument for the motion of the earth. (John Lear, *Kepler's Dream*, p.89).

John Lear who compiled with notes the text of the *Dream*, stresses this purpose:

> Therefore, Kepler reasoned, by taking people vicariously to the moon and standing them seemingly still there, he could show them the earth in motion. (p. 66).

Had Kepler actually gone to the moon it is likely he would have been disappointed. The Apollo astronauts are not very specific on this point!

The Solar System Suddenly Becomes Much Bigger

Kepler's calculations notwithstanding, the modern concept of the size of the solar system and more specifically the *astronomical unit* (the earth to sun distance) would not be approximated to the modern calculation until later. But, *not much later*! The astronomical unit (AU) is defined by the International Astronomical Union as the *mean distance* between the earth and the sun over one earth orbit. Until 1976 the astronomical unit was defined by the IAU as the length of the *semi-major axis* of the Earth's elliptical orbit around the Sun. The AU is currently said to be about 149,597,870.7 kilometres, (92,955,801 miles).

In the 2nd century AD, Ptolemy estimated the mean distance of the sun as 1,210 times the Earth radius. If we use the current equatorial radius of 3,963 miles, Ptolemy's computation would give a distance of 4,795,230 miles from the earth to the sun.

This figure of less than five million miles did not increase during the days of Copernicus and Tycho Brahe. In fact it lessened somewhat.

> After Greek astronomy was transmitted to the medieval Islamic world, astronomers made some changes to Ptolemy's cosmological model, but did not greatly change his estimate of

the Earth-Sun distance. For example, in his introduction to Ptolemaic astronomy, al-Farghānī gave a mean solar distance of 1,170 Earth radii, while in his zij, al-Battānī used a mean solar distance of 1,108 Earth radii. Subsequent astronomers, such as al-Bīrūnī used similar values. Later in Europe, Copernicus and Tycho Brahe also used comparable figures (1,142 Earth radii and 1,150 Earth radii), and so Ptolemy's approximate Earth-Sun distance survived through the 16th century.   *(Wikipedia* sourced from Albert van Helden, *Measuring the Universe: Cosmic Dimensions from Aristarchus to Halley*, pp. 15–27).

Kepler in the *Rudolphine Tables* (1627) was the first to propose that Ptolemy's estimate must be significantly too low, and increased the distance to nearly 3500 earth radii. His laws of planetary motion provided astronomers with a basis to calculate the proportionate distances of the planets from the Sun, but not their actual distances.

As *NASA* recounts:

> Tycho Brahe estimated the distance between the Sun and the Earth at 8 million kilometers (5 million miles). Later, Johannes Kepler estimated the AU was at 24 million kilometers (15 million miles). In 1672, Giovanni Cassini made a much better estimate by using Mars. By observing Mars from Paris and having a colleague, Jean Richer, also observe Mars at the same time in French Guiana in South America, Cassini determined the parallax of Mars. From that Cassini was able to calculate the distance from Earth to Mars, and then the distance from Earth to the Sun. Cassini calculated the AU to be at 140 million kilometers (87 million miles), which is lower, but very close to the modern day number.
> (neo.jpl.nasa.gov/glossary).

It is curious that by using triangulation, astronomers (including Copernicus) from the Second to the to the early Seventeenth century figured the astronomical unit to be only about 5 million miles, and that after that, also my using triangulation, it grew to near its present 93 million miles. Even with bringing Mars into the equation it is remarkable that there could be such a large variation.

As shown below, while radar is used for determining planetary distances, it cannot give the AU. A radar beam cannot be "bounced" back to earth from the sun.

How Planetary Distance Has Been Measured

Keeping in mind the quantum increase in the AU that took place after Tycho Brahe, the following explains the factors used today in determining planetary measurements. These include trigonometry (triangulation), radar, and the earlier planetary laws founded upon Kepler.

> Very precise measurements of the relative positions of the inner planets can be made by radar and by telemetry from space probes. As with all radar measurements, these rely on measuring the time taken for light to be reflected from an object. These measured positions are then compared with those calculated by the laws of celestial mechanics: the calculated positions are often referred to as an ephemeris (from the Greek word *ephemeros* "daily", is a table of values that gives the positions of astronomical objects

in the sky at a given time or times). These are usually calculated in astronomical units. (*Wikipedia*).

NASA says:

> Johannes Kepler... knew that the movement of the planets around the Sun could be described by physics - and in mathematical terms. The closer the planet was to the Sun, the faster it moved. Conversely, farther planets orbited the Sun more slowly. Knowing this, he was able to connect the average distance of a planet from the Sun with the time it takes that planet to orbit the Sun once. Though he wasn't able to come up with distance measurements in kilometres, Kepler was able to order the planets by distance and to figure out their proportional distances. For example, he knew that Mars was about 1.5 times farther from the Sun than the Earth.

Parallax

If you hold your finger in front of your face, close one eye and look with the other, then switch eyes, you'll see your finger seem to "shift " with respect to more distant objects behind it. This is because your eyes are separated from each other by a distance of a few inches - so each eye sees the finger in front of you from a slightly different angle. The amount your finger seems to shift is called its "parallax".

In the late 17th century, Giovanni Cassini used the parallax technique to measure the distance to Mars. Cassini knew that a larger parallax would be easier to measure - but this required a larger baseline (i.e. the baseline would be like the distance between your eyes) He took measurements of the position of Mars from Paris and sent a fellow astronomer to French Guiana in South America to do the same. This gave him a baseline of several thousand kilometres - using geometry, he was able to calculate a distance for Mars that is only 7% off today's more precise measurements!

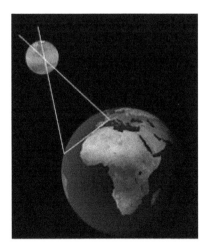

Even with modern technology, measuring distances by parallax isn't trivial - and the errors can be big - as we can see from Cassini's measurement of the Earth-Mars distance.

Radar

One of the most accurate ways to measure the distances to the planets is by bouncing radar off them, or sending a spacecraft there, which can send a radio signal back to the Earth that can be timed. Radar is essentially microwave electromagnetic radiation (microwaves fall under the radio spectrum). Since electromagnetic radiation, in all of its forms, is light, we know that radar travels at the speed of light - 2.99×10^5 km/s. Simply, distance traveled is equal to the time multiplied by the velocity. If we bounce radar off a planet, and measure the time it takes the signal to go there and back, we can use this information to calculate the distance of the planet.

Distant Solar System Objects

There are other modern methods to calculate the distances to objects on the fringes of our Solar System, like Kuiper Belt or Scattered Disc Objects. However, these techniques are often based on those Kepler employed! Several observations of the object's position in the sky are recorded, which are then used to determine the orbit of the object - then the position of the object along each point can be calculated. (heasarc.gsfc.nasa.gov).

Astronomynotes.com gives the following illustrations in a heliocentric solar system of the use of triangulation in measurement of planetary distance. It seems strange that while not mentioning that Copernicus estimated the astronomical unit to be less than 5 million miles, yet at the same time he was able to "determine approximate distances between the planets."

Several hundred years ago Copernicus was able to determine approximate distances between the planets through trigonometry. The distances were all found relative to the distance between the Earth and the Sun, the *astronomical unit.* Kepler refined these measurements to take into account the elliptical orbits. However, they did not know how large an astronomical unit was.

To establish an absolute distance scale, the actual distance to one of the planets had to be measured. Distances to Venus and Mars were measured from the parallax effect by observers at different parts of the Earth when the planets were closest to the Earth.

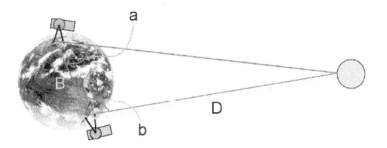

Triangulation gives the distance: measure angles
(a & b) and distance (B) between the observation
points. Derive the distance (D) to the nearby object.

When the length of the base line (B), and the observation angles (a and b) are known, then the distance (D) to the object is known.

Knowing how far apart the observers were from each other and coordinating the observation times, astronomers could determine the distance to a planet. The slight difference in its position on the sky due to observing the planet from different positions gave the planet's distance from trigonometry. The state-of-the-art measurements still had a large margin of uncertainty. The last major effort using these techniques was in the 1930's. Parallax observations of an asteroid, called Eros, passing close to Earth were used to fix the value of the astronomical unit at 150 million kilometres.

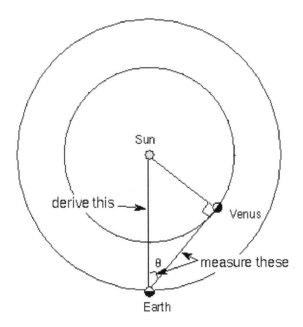

Measuring the angle θ between Venus and the Sun and
the distance between Earth and Venus enables us to find the
distance between the Earth and the Sun using trigonometry.

Measuring the angle q between Venus and the Sun, and the distance between earth and Venus enables us to find the distance between the earth and the sun using trigonometry.

> With the invention of radar, the distance to Venus could be determined very precisely. By timing how long it takes the radar beam travelling at the speed of light to travel the distance to an object and back, the distance to the object can be found from distance = (speed of light) × (total time)/2. The total time is halved to get just the distance from the Earth to the object. Using trigonometry, astronomers now know that the *astronomical unit* =149,597,892 kilometres. This incredible degree of accuracy is possible because the speed of light is known very precisely and very accurate clocks are used. You cannot use radar to determine the distance to the Sun directly because the Sun has no solid surface to reflect the radar efficiently. (astronomynotes.com)

The observed movement of Venus across the Sun is called its *transit*. As the following from *Wikipedia* explains, this became a means of seeking to estimate the AU. Yet as the following also indicates, the pursuit of the astronomical unit has been a difficult exercse.

> A somewhat more accurate estimate can be obtained by observing the transit of Venus. By measuring the transit in two different locations, one can accurately calculate the parallax of Venus, and from the relative distance of the Earth and Venus from the Sun, the solar parallax α (which cannot be measured directly). Jeremiah Horrocks had attempted to produce an estimate based on his observation of the 1639 transit (published in 1662), giving a solar parallax of 15 arcseconds…The solar parallax is related to the Earth–Sun distance as measured in Earth radii by:

> The smaller the solar parallax, the greater the distance between the Sun and the Earth: a solar parallax of 15" is equivalent to an Earth–Sun distance of 13,750 Earth radii [over 54 million miles].

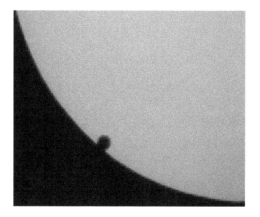

Transits of Venus across the face of the Sun were, for a long time, the best method of measuring the astronomical unit, despite the difficulties. These included the rarity of the transits and also the "black drop effect", (a small black "teardrop" appears to connect Venus' disk to the circumferenc of the Sun, making it impossible to accurately time the exact moment of second or third contact).

Jean Richer and Giovanni Domenico Cassini measured the parallax of Mars between Paris and Cayenne in French Guiana when Mars was at its closest to Earth in 1672. They arrived at a figure for the solar parallax of 9½", equivalent to an Earth–Sun distance of about 22,000 Earth radii. They were also the first astronomers to have access to an accurate and reliable value for the radius of the Earth [in 200 BC Eratosthenes estimate was only 16.8 kilometres off], which had been measured by their colleague Jean Picard in 1669 as 3,269 thousand *toises* [varying from 2 metres or slightly less]. Another colleague, Ole Rømer, discovered the finite speed of light in 1676: the speed was so great that it was usually quoted as the time required for light to travel from the Sun to the Earth, or "light time per unit distance", a convention that is still followed by astronomers today.

A better method for observing Venus transits was devised by James Gregory and published in his Optica Promata (1663). It was strongly advocated by Edmond Halley and was applied to the transits of Venus observed in 1761 and 1769, and then again in 1874 and 1882. Transits of Venus occur in pairs, but less than one pair every century, and the observations of the transits in 1761 and 1769 was an unprecedented international scientific operation. Despite the Seven Years' War, dozens of astronomers were dispatched to observing points around the world at great expense and personal danger: several of them died in the endeavour. The various results were collated by Jérôme Lalande to give a figure for the solar parallax of 8.6″.

Another method involved determining the constant of aberration [a phenomenon which produces an apparent motion of celestial objects about their real locations], and Simon Newcomb gave great weight to this method when deriving his widely accepted value of 8.80″ for the solar parallax (close to the modern value of 8.794143″), although Newcomb also used data from the transits of Venus. Newcomb also collaborated with A. A. Michelson to measure the speed of light with Earth-based equipment: combined with the constant of aberration (which is related to the light time per unit distance) this gave the first direct measurement of the Earth–Sun distance in kilometres. Newcomb's value for the solar parallax was incorporated into the first international system of astronomical constants in 1896, and which remained in place for the calculation of ephemerides [a table of values that gives the positions of astronomical objects] until 1964. The name "astronomical unit" appears first to have been used in 1903. (*Wikipedia*, with sources).

Direct radar measurements of the distances to Venus and Mars became available in the early 1960s. Along with improved measurements of the speed of light, these showed that Newcomb's values for the solar parallax and the constant of aberration were inconsistent with one another. (Mikhailov, A. A. "The Constant of Aberration and the Solar Parallax", *Sov. Astron.* 7, 6: pp.737–39).

In the seventy years after Tycho Brahe, the astronomical unit grew exponentially. And, this apparently without any significant advance or alteration to the observations he had amassed. Again, it is strange that by using triangulation, astronomers (including Copernicus) from the Second to the to the early Seventeenth century figured the astronomical unit to be only about 5 million miles, and that after that, also by using triangulation, it grew near to the present 93 million miles. How could one basic means of measurement (even with additional applications) allow for such a huge variation? The above gives a fairly full explanation, but again we are bound to ask whether the changeover from geocentricity to heliocentricity had any bearing upon this increase in distance. The Tychonic system is adaptable to both the small and large distance view.

Galileo and the Telescope

Galileo Galilei (1564-1642) was an Italian physicist, mathematician and astronomer who played a major role in the development and use of the telescope, and in the the general acceptance of heliocentricity. He has been called the "father of modern observational astronomy". His contributions include the telescopic confirmation of the phases of Venus, the discovery of the four largest satellites of Jupiter (named the Galilean moons in his honour), and the observation and analysis of sunspots.

After 1610 he began to publicly support the heliocentric view and was denounced to the Roman Inquisition in 1615. In the following year the Catholic Church declared heliocentrism to be "false and contrary to Scripture" (Michael Sharratt, *Galileo: Decisive Innovator*, pp. 127-131). Galileo was warned to abandon his support for the idea, which he promised to do, and would refer to it only as a theory and computational device. When he later defended his views in his famous work, *Dialogue Concerning the Two Chief World Systems*, published in 1632, he was tried by the Inquisition, and found "vehemently suspect of heresy". He was forced to recant, and though living with a state pension and in a comfortable villa outside of Florence, his movements were restricted by the Pope. Galileo's *Dialogue* was banned, and publication of any current or future works forbidden (Stillman Drake, *Galileo At Work*, p. 367). By 1638 he was completely blind, but continued to receive visitors until his death in 1642, aged 77.

Galileo's use of the telescope began in 1609, and along with the Englishman Thomas Harriot and others, was among the first to use and develop this instrument. It was known as a Refractor (also Dioptic) which uses lenses, and gets its name from the image being formed by refracting or bending the incoming light. Refractors are distinguished from the later Reflectors (Catoptrics) which use mirrors, and the Combined Lens-Mirror Systems (Catadioptrics).

The first practical refracting telescopes appeared in the Netherlands in about 1608, and were credited to Hans Lippershey and Zacharias Janssen, spectacle-makers, and also Jacob Metius. Galileo, happening to be in Venice at or about May of 1609, heard of the invention and constructed a version of his own which he presented to the public and governing leadership of Venice.

Galileo Showing the Doge of Venice How to Use the Telescope

Galileo's best telescope magnified objects about 30 times. Several design flaws in its design, such as the shape of the lens and the narrow field of view, meant that the images were blurred and distorted. Nevertheless it was still good enough for him to view the phases of Venus, the craters on the Moon and the four moons orbiting Jupiter. The Keplerian Telescope, invented by Johannes Kepler in 1611, was an improvement on Galileo's design in its use of a convex lens as the eyepiece instead of Galileo's concave lens.

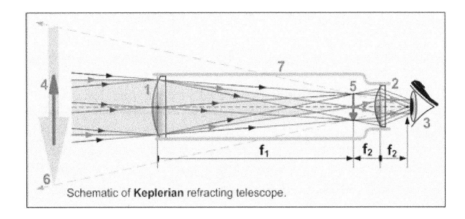

Schematic of **Keplerian** refracting telescope.

All refracting telescopes use the same principles. The combination of an objective lens **1,** and the eyepiece **2,** is used to gather more light than the human eye could collect on its own, and then focus it **5,** and present the viewer with a brighter, clearer, and magnified virtual image **6**. (adapted from *Wikipedia*).

Galileo's "Proofs" for Heliocentricity – <u>No Proof</u>

Today the impression is given that wth the advent of Galileo's telescopic observations convincing evidence was presented for the changeover to heliocentricity. A step by step look at his evidence will show that this was not the case. It is true that some of his observations made things more difficult for the Ptolemaic view of the solar system. The same could not be said however for the Tychonic system which could fit in quite readily with Galileo's observations. This simple fact must certainly explain why Galileo in presenting his evidence ignores Tycho and directs his fire solely against Ptolemy. This is the point to bear in mind when viewing Galileo's "proofs": <u>He does not address the Tychonic system</u>, nor does he accept Kepler's eliptical orbits which by all accounts were formulated from Tycho's observational data. It is strictly Copernicus against Ptolemy, and circular orbits against circular orbits. And this not withstanding that the Copernican system with its many epicycles was arguably as complex as the Ptolemaic.

As Hutchison explains:

> The bulk of Galileo's argument, and all that portion of it that utilizes novel empirical data, is directed against those who do not accept the Tychonic system as the best available

geocentric comsomogy, and thus has no bearing on the question whether the earth moves. As many of Galileo's opponents were already willing to accept the Tychonic arrangement, Galileo's evidence falls lamely to the side of his true target. (Keith Hutchison, "Sunspots, Galileo and the Orbit of the Earth", *Isis* 81.1, p.68).

Galileo was not the first to study the heavenly bodies through a telescope but he was the first to publish his findings. His initial observations were published in his popular 1610 book "The Starry Messenger" (*Sidereus Nuncius*). The Jesuits whom he needed to convince, however, were not impressed. And, with good reason!

1. Jupiter's Four Moons

Much is made of Galileo's discovery of Jupiter's moons as an argument for heliocentricity.

> On 7 January 1610 Galileo observed with his telescope what he described at the time as "three fixed stars, totally invisible by their smallness," all close to Jupiter, and lying on a straight line through it. Observations on subsequent nights showed that the positions of these "stars" relative to Jupiter were changing in a way that would have been inexplicable if they had really been fixed stars…Within a few days he concluded that they were orbiting Jupiter: He had discovered three of Jupiter's four largest satellites (moons). He discovered the fourth on 13 January.

> Once Galileo realized what he had seen a few days later, his observations of the satellites of Jupiter created a revolution in astronomy that reverberates to this day: a planet with smaller planets orbiting it did not conform to the principles of Aristotelian Cosmology, which held that all heavenly bodies should circle the Earth, and many astronomers and philosophers initially refused to believe that Galileo could have discovered such a thing. His observations were confirmed by the observatory of Christopher Clavius and he received a hero's welcome when he visited Rome in 1611. (*Wikipedia* with sources).

To say that Galileo's discovery of these moons "created a revolution in astronomy that reverberates to this day" is an example of the kind of exaggeration that accompanied the changeover to heliocentricity. It also demonstrates how much was made of little, and how thin the observational evidence was.

It was on this page that Galileo first noted an observation of the moons of Jupiter. Galileo published a full description in *Sidereus Nuncius* in March 1610

The Aristotelians maintained that the earth could not be in motion around the sun for the reason that it would have to drag the moon along with it. This in their thinking was an impossibility. Galileo argued that if Jupiter could drag its moons in a journey around the sun, the same would be true for the earth. This is a false analogy. Jupiter having four moons may have upset Aristotelian Cosmology but it had no direct bearing as to whether or not the earth was moving or was in the center of the cosmos. The Jesuits in their debates with Galileo correctly understood that this was not a proof for the motion of the earth. It takes a great deal of overstatement to call it *a revolution in astronomy that reverberates to this day*.

2. The Phases of Venus

Galileo's discovery of the phases of Venus was considered his most conclusive evidence for a sun-centred solar system.

From September 1610, Galileo observed that Venus exhibited a full set of phases similar to that of the Moon. The heliocentric model of the solar system developed by Nicolaus Copernicus predicted that all phases would be visible since the orbit of Venus around the Sun would cause its illuminated hemisphere to face the Earth when it was on the opposite side of the Sun and to face away from the Earth when it was on the Earth-side of the Sun. On the other hand, in Ptolemy's geocentric model it was impossible for any of the planets' orbits to intersect the spherical shell carrying the Sun. Traditionally the orbit of Venus was placed entirely on the near side of the Sun, where it could exhibit only crescent and new phases. It was, however, also possible to place it entirely on the far side of the Sun, where it could exhibit only gibbous and full phases. After Galileo's telescopic observations of the crescent, gibbous and full phases of Venus, therefore, this Ptolemaic model became untenable. Thus in the early 17th century as a result of his discovery the great majority of astronomers converted to one of the various geo-heliocentric planetary models, such as the Tychonic, Capellan and Extended Capellan models, each either with or without a daily rotating Earth. These all had the virtue of explaining the phases of Venus... Galileo's discovery of the phases of Venus was thus arguably his most empirically practically influential contribution to the two-stage transition from full geocentrism to full heliocentrism via geo-heliocentrism. (*Wikipedia*, with sources).

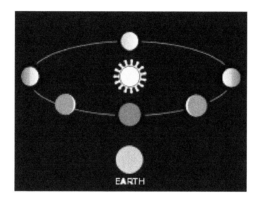

The phases of Venus, observed by Galileo in 1610

While the Tyconic system with circular orbits fully accounts for the phases of Venus, (a fact not mentioned by Galileo), the Ptolemaic system, despite the above, can also show the same if its orbits are eliptical rather than circular.

> Galileo incorrectly maintained that the Ptolemaic model could not account for the phases of Venus and Mercury. Actually, his argument is correct as long as one insists on circular orbits; but if one allows for elliptical orbits in the Ptolemaic model then the argument falls flat... (Bouw, *Geocentricity*, pp. 188,189).

This "strongest proof" was not a proof at all.

3. Sunspots and the Sun's Rotation

As with Kepler who is his *Astronomia Nova* saw the sun as a rotating cartwheel that pushed the planets around in their orbits, so Galileo believed that the Sun was the driving force of the solar system. If the Sun at the center were shown to rotate, it would then be able to drag the planets around itself. Further, if the sun were rotating it would be likely that the earth was also rotating. This was therefore but another agument from analogy.

Galileo's observation of sunspots indicated that the sun rotated about once each month.

Galileo observed the Sun through his telescope and saw that the Sun had dark patches on it that we now call sunspots (he eventually went blind, perhaps from damage suffered by looking at the Sun with his telescope). Furthermore, he observed motion of the sunspots indicating that the Sun was rotating on an axis. These "blemishes" on the Sun were contrary to the doctrine of an unchanging perfect substance in the heavens, and <u>the rotation of the Sun made it less strange that the Earth might rotate on an axis too</u>, as required in the Copernican model. Both represented new facts that were unknown to Aristotle and Ptolemy. (csep10.phys.utk.edu/astr161/lect/history/galileo.html emphasis mine).

In his 1612 *Discourse* (2nd Edition) Galileo wrote:

> …at last, my repeated observations have made me certain that those spots are substances contiguous with the surface of the solar body, and that many are produced and then dissolved continuously, some lasting for very brief intervals of time, and others for longer times, and they are carried around by the rotation of the Sun on itself, completing its period in approximately one month, an occurrence in itself most great and important for its consequences. (Wilbur Applebaum, and Renzo Baldasso, *Galileo and Kepler on the Sun as Planetary Mover*, p. 186).

If the sun moved (spun on an axis), Galileo reasoned it must also be the *mover*, and the force dragging the other planets around in their orbital paths. Again, this is but argument from analogy rather than clear demonstratable evidence. This led, however, to a further argument concerning the sun which we will reserve for the last.

In 1632 Galileo published what he felt were his most "convincing" arguments. David Topper writes:

> Near the end of the *Dialogue concerning the Two Chief World Systems* (1632), in his summing-up argument, Galileo puts forth what he believes are three "very convincing" arguments that constitute "strong evidences in favor of the Copernican system" (Gallieo p. 462). They are: the explanation of the planetary retrograde motion, the motion of sunspots, and the theory of the tides. ("I know that what I am saying is rather obscure… On Clarifying a Passage in Galileo's *Dialogue*," *Centaurus*, 42.4, p. 288).

4. Planetary Retrograde Motion

From the northern hemisphere we see the sun, moon, stars and planets moving east to west across the sky. We also detect that over the course of a year the sun and planets "have not kept up" but have regressed somewhat to the east against the background stars.

The so-called inner planets, Venus and Mercury, are seen travelling with the sun, never far from it, and appear to move from one side of the sun to the other. The outer planets: Mars, Jupiter and Saturn (in Galileo's time) "break rank" in the prevailing westerly movement and periodically appear to move easterly against the background stars before returning again westerly. This is called their retrograde motion, and gives the "planets" their names: *wanderers* (from Greek and Latin).

Ptolemy explained retrograde motion by assuming that each planet moved in a circle called an epicycle, whose center was in turn carried around the earth in a circular orbit called a deferent…The fact that the inferior planets (Venus and Mercury) never stray far from the sun was explained by the provision that the centers of their epicycles always had to lie on the line connecting the earth and sun.

In the final version of his system Ptolemy modified the postulate of uniform motion in order to explain the variations in the apparent speeds of the planets. He found that these variations could be reproduced most conveniently by displacing the earth from the center of the deferent to a point called the eccentric. He then assumed that the motion of the center of the epicycle along the deferent appeared uniform, not from the center of the deferent or from the eccentric, but from a third point symmetrically displaced from the eccentric, called the equant. ("The Fundamentals of the Ptolemaic System," *The Columbia Encyclopedia, Infoplease.com*).

Galileo sought to contrast the complexity of this arrangement with the "relatively simple" system of Copernicus. Regarding the outward planets he explained that as they had orbits that were outside that of the Earth, they moved more slowly. The Earth's orbit, therefore, overtook them from time to time, and when it did, they appeared to be moving backwards in the sky.

As seen above in the discussion of Copernicus' system, Gingerich and others show that the system Galileo put forward was any thing but simple! Copernicus did not need to use Ptolemy's equant; but he did use epicycles orbiting on a deferent. Though his epicycles were smaller (he called them "epicycletes"), he in fact used more than Ptolemy. One writer goes so far as to say that he used "twice as many". (O. Neugebauer, *The Exact Sciences in Antiquity*, p. 204).

The Tyconic model without epicycles, deferents or equants and using eliptical orbits fully accounts for retrogade motion. A point of which Galileo was silent.

5. Tides

Galileo held passionately to the idea that the tides were a clear evidence of heliocentricity and the earth's motion. As the following shows, however, his tidal theory was early shown to be fundamentally in error.

Cardinal Bellarmine had written in 1615 that the Copernican system could not be defended without "a true physical demonstration that the sun does not circle the earth but the earth circles the sun." Galileo considered his theory of the tides to provide the required physical proof of the motion of the earth. This theory was so important to Galileo that he originally intended to entitle his *Dialogue on the Two Chief World Systems* the *Dialogue on the Ebb and Flow of the Sea*. The reference to tides was removed by order of the Inquisition.

For Galileo, the tides were caused by the sloshing back and forth of water in the seas as a point on the Earth's surface speeded up and slowed down because of the Earth's rotation on its axis and revolution around the Sun. Galileo circulated his first account of the tides in 1616, addressed to Cardinal Orsini. His theory gave the first insight into the importance of the shapes of ocean basins in the size and timing of tides; he correctly accounted, for instance, for the negligible tides halfway along the Adriatic Sea compared to those at the ends. As a general account of the cause of tides, however, his theory was a failure.

If this theory were correct, there would be only one high tide per day. Galileo and his contemporaries were aware of this inadequacy because there are two daily high tides at Venice instead of one, about twelve hours apart. Galileo dismissed this anomaly as the result of several secondary causes, including the shape of the sea, its depth, and other factors. Against the assertion that Galileo was deceptive in making these arguments, Albert Einstein expressed the opinion that Galileo developed his "fascinating arguments" and accepted them uncritically out of a desire for physical proof of the motion of the Earth.

Galileo dismissed as a "useless fiction" the idea, held by his contemporary Johannes Kepler, that the moon caused the tides. Galileo also refused to accept Kepler's elliptical orbits of the planets, considering the circle the "perfect" shape for planetary orbits (*Wikipedia* with sources).

6. Sunspot Trajectories Require a Complex Motion of the Sun in the Ptolemaic System

Galileo argued that sunspot movement across the face of the Sun indicated that the earth was both rotating on its axis and orbiting the sun. He said that if the sun where orbiting the earth, its

movement would have to be more complex than could be reasonably expected and that four motions would be required.

1. A monthly rotation of the sun on its axis.
2. An annual (counter clockwise) revolution around the earth, on the ecliptic.
3. A daily (clockwise) revolution around the earth, parallel to the celestial equator.
4. A conical motion, around its center, since the sun remains tilted over its orbit. (Topper, David. "I know that what I am saying is rather obscure… On Clarifying a Passage in Galileo's *Dialogue*," *Centaurus* 2000, Vol. 42, p. 291).

This is of course not a proof, but rather an argument from "simpler is better". The Bible says that only one of the two bodies is moving: the sun. Galileo divided motion between the sun and the earth, but with two motions to the earth (rotation and revolution) and one to the sun (rotation). He argued that by reducing the number of motions from four to three his system was less complex and therefore evidence on the side of heliocentricity. We must ask, however, whether Galileo was overstating this argument and whether sunspots can convincingly demonstrate any motion in addition to that of the sun's rotation.

That the sun has a complex rotation beyond what Galileo would have known is seen in the following answer to the question: *Does the Sun rotate? Are we seeing the same face of the Sun all the time?*

The Answer

Yes, the Sun does rotate. We can observe this by observing sunspots. All sunspots move across the face of the Sun. This motion is part of the general rotation of the Sun on its axis. Observations also indicate that the Sun does not rotate as a solid body, but it spins differentially. That means that it rotates faster at the equator of the Sun and slower at its poles. (The gas giants Jupiter and Saturn also have differential rotation.) The movements of the sunspots indicate that the Sun rotates once every 27 days at the equator, but only once in 31 days at the poles. (Padi Boyd imagine.gsfc.nasa.gov/docs/ask).

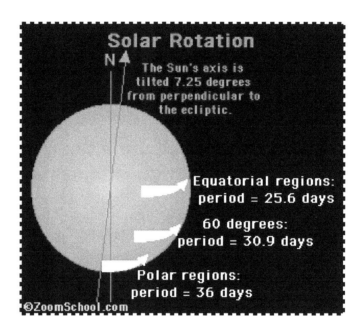

Therefore with this *differential* rotation it is best to let the sun rather than supposed movement of the earth explain:

> …annually periodic seasonal variations of sunspot trajectories across the sun's disc. They appear to oscillate above and below its apparent equator over the course of the four seasons…(See p. 345-56 of Stillman Drake's 1967 *Dialogue concerning the two chief world systems*. But see Drake's *Sunspots, Sizzi and Scheiner'* in his 1970 *Galileo Studies* for its critical discussion of Galileo's misleading presentation of this phenomenon).

In short, Galileo saw the suns movement, not the earth's.

> *He maketh his sun to rise on the evil and on the good, and sendeth rain on the just and on the unjust.* Matthew 5:45.

> *He appointed the moon for seasons: the sun knoweth his going down.* Psalm 104:19.

Heliocentricity Advances Despite Scripture and the Failure of Galileo's "Proofs"

At the the time of Galileo's death in 1642 nothing approaching a proof had been found that demonstrated a rotating earth orbiting a central sun. Despite all that is attributed to him on behalf of heliocentricity, the reality of the case is that his "proofs" were not "proofs" and fell far short of a convincing demonstation.

Keith Hutchison writes:

> Historians are nowadays in fairly wide agreement that though Galileo produced all sorts of important reasons for rejecting the views of his geocentric opponents [Ptolemy not Tycho as Hutchison shows], and thus gave his own opinions powerful indirect support, <u>he never managed to devise a direct demonstration that the earth is in motion</u>. We do not take this view because of some deep-seated skepticism about the possibilities of achieving proof in the empirical sciences—because, that is, of some philosophical preference that prevents us from recognizing the merits of Galileo's case. Instead, <u>we see his arguments as falling so short of their aim that they can be dismissed</u> without our needing to think deeply about what would constitute a rational demonstration that the earth moves. ("Sunspots, Galileo, and the Orbit of the Earth," *Isis* 81.1, p. 68, emphasis mine).

This is the key to understanding the history of the rise of heliocentricity: It became established in the centers of learning *without a single demonstrable proof*. In this it was the forerunner of that other deception, Darwinism, which a little over two centuries after Galileo would accomplish the same swift march into these same centers of learning *without demonstrable proof*. Geocentricity (in its Tychonic form) went almost immediately into terminal decline. Quoting again from Christine Schofield:

> Some acceptance of the Tychonic system persisted through the 17th century and in places until the early 18th century…But in Germany, Holland, and England, the Tychonic system "vanished from the literature much earlier". (Christine Schofield, *The Tychonic and Semi-Tychonic World Systems*, pp. 41,43).

Newton "Axiomizes" Heliocentricity - <u>Proof Remains Elusive</u>

Copernicus, Kepler and Galileo presented their ideas on behalf of heliocentricity, but as we have shown were unable to give demonstrable proof. We now add a fourth name, history's "premier scientist": Issac Newton (1642-1727). Newton would take the heliocentric theories of his predecessors and use them in synthesis with his three laws of motion and his law of universal gravitation. Heliocentricity and especially Kepler's laws of planetary motion were therefore *axiomized*. This gave heliocentrictiy a near universal credibility and established it at the heart of scientific thinking.

The following gives a summary view of how Newton is understood to have unified heliocentric astronomy with physics:

Kepler had proposed three Laws of Planetary motion based on the systematics that he found in Brahe's data. These Laws were supposed to apply only to the motions of the planets; they said nothing about any other motion in the Universe. Further, they were purely empirical: they worked, but no one knew a fundamental reason WHY they should work.

Newton changed all of that. First, he demonstrated that the motion of objects on the Earth could be described by three new Laws of motion, and then he went on to show that Kepler's three Laws of Planetary Motion were but special cases of Newton's three Laws if a force of a particular kind (what we now know to be the gravitational force) were postulated to exist between all objects in the Universe having mass. In fact, Newton went even further: he showed that Kepler's Laws of planetary motion were only approximately correct, and supplied the quantitative corrections that with careful observations proved to be valid.
(http://csep10.phys.utk.edu/astr161/lect/history/newton.html).

Newton's system of mechanics was published in his famous *The Principia*. Yet despite the extent of his formulations, and the credibility he gave to the heliocentrric system, he did not present anything that approached the long sought after *demonstratable proof* .

Newton, himself, did not offer any such "proofs" but actually countered some which had been proposed. This is not to say that Newton may have viewed such "proofs" as impossible when it comes to the motion of the earth for he clearly searched for some which would settle the issue either way; but Newton did not, himself, offer any such proofs. (Bouw, *Geocentricity*, p. 225).

The Heliocentric System Becomes a Fact <u>Without Proof</u>

With Newton we come to the end of *Part III: What History Records*. Given the quantum leap that took place in the acceptantance of heliocentricity, it is a curious fact that the *leap* was taken without *demonstratable proof*. Theories and arguments were presented. The search for hard evidence could not have been more diligent. But, curiously, conclusive proof remained elusive and out of reach.

It is also to be stressed that from Copernicus to Newton (and before) no one had gathered anything remotely approaching Tycho Brahe's observational data. Even given the disadvantage of being a pre-telescope astronomer, the breadth and accuracy of his work are a wonder in this day. This vast catalog presented, in the view of the great man, a clear demonstration of the geostatic solar system.

The Subjugating of Scripture to Physical Laws

The changeover from Geocentricity to Heliocentricity saw the formulation of many of the "laws" of physics. Their formulation, in fact, was frequently a direct consequence of the Copernican revolution. These laws and constants may (or may not!) reflect the realities of how God's creation works. If they are true then they are the Lord's servants. He is not subject to them and may at any time override them. It is therefore a mistake to subjugate the Bible to the laws of physics.

Isaac Newton's law concerning the Center of Mass cannot therefore not be used as an argument against the sun moving around the earth. In fact the earth may be at the center of the mass of the universe, and of which mass the sun is only a tiny part. The same could be said for the speed of light constant. God's workings are not subjugated to that or any other constant.

Newton was to base his *Universal Law of Gravitation* on Kepler's *Three Laws of Planetary Motion*. Yet few Christians have grasped the fact that this law by stating that gravity is innate and inherent within matter displaces Christ *in whom all things consist* (hold together). Colossians 1:17.

Or as Robert Sungenis writes:

> As a background, satellites are an anomaly for scientists. They know they work, but they are not quite sure how. In a similar way, they know that gravity works, but they don't now how. All they really know about gravity is that its force is proportional to the inverse square of the distance, but they don't know what "caused" gravity. Newton himself admitted this. The only thing Newton did is measure the force of gravity and put it into a mathematical formula, not explain the nature of gravity. Unfortunately, most scientists today think that merely because they have a mathematical formula to explain the results of a certain phenomenon, this necessarily means they have discovered the reality, but that is not the case at all. (*About Scientific and Theological Aspects of Geocentricity*, p. 5).

Newton himself said:

> It is inconceivable that inanimate brute matter should, without mediation of something else, which is not material, operate upon, and affect other matter without mutual contact. (***Four Letters From Sir Isaac Newton to Doctor Bentley Containing Some Arguments in Proof of a Deity, cited by Bouw, Geocentricity, p. 221***).

Therefore beyond what Scripture reveals, there are clear limitations to man's knowledge of the *ordinances of celestial motion.*

- Knowest thou the ordinances of heaven? canst thou set the dominion thereof in the earth? Job 38:33.
- *Then I beheld all the work of God, that a man cannot find out the work that is done under the sun: because though a man labour to seek it out, yet he shall not find it; yea farther; though a wise man think to know it, yet shall he not be able to find it. Ecclesiastes 8:17.*

And while the world of academia may see things as expressed in Alexander Pope's lines, the Christian should view all things from the standpoint of the Bible.

> *Nature and Nature's laws*
> *Lay hid in night:*
> *God said, Let Newton be!*
> *And all was light*

Knowledge that does not acknowledge God and the Bible will soon become corrupted. As heliocentricism (and shortly acentricism) became an assumed fact, it can be shown that a number of associated laws and constants are an accommodation to that assumption.

Part IV: What True Science Reveals

After Newton and leading up to the Twentieth Century a number of new evidences were put forward on behalf of heliocentricity. These, however, could be answered just as readily within the Tychonic system. Certainly, and especially in view of the famous Michelson-Morley experiment, there was not enough further evidence to justify the fundamental change that had taken place. It was much like the paucity of evidence presented to justify the acceptance of evolution. For the Bible believer this should not be too great of a surprise! Given the fallen heart of man and that the god of this world hath blinded the minds of them that believe not (II Cor. 4:4), it does not take a great deal of persuasion to get the world moving in the wrong direction. Nor did it take a great deal of persuasion to get the world to believe that the earth beneath its feet was moving.

By the beginning of the 19th Century the last of the "holdouts" among Europe's leading astronomers (the French Cassini dynasty) finally moved over to the heliocentricity side. But still, despite a number of key experiments during and toward the latter part of the 19th Century, conclusive demonstration of the earth's motion remained wanting. Results "stubbornly and persistently" pointed in the opposite direction. Notable among these experiments was that conducted by George Airy in 1871. As with his predecessors, this Astronomer Royal at Greenwich failed to demonstrate an earth in motion. This was known as Airy's Failure.

In 1881, however, a crisis point was reached. The Michelson-Morley experiment was conducted in Berlin, and again six years later with greater precision in Cleveland, Ohio. Since then it has been conducted many times and with ever greater refinement, and always points to an earth that is motionless (or nearly so). As everyone after all this time (in the 1880s) "knew" that the earth was in motion, an answer to this troubling anomaly must now be found. A "bridging" solution was proposed in the strange Fitzgerald Contraction theory, but a full answer was not attempted for another two decades with the appearance of Einstein and his Special Theory of Relativity.

In all of this we have seen how that an idea can be presented. Nobody knows for certain whether or not it is true. In time assumptions are strengthened. Arguments against are marginalized. Mathematical formulas are produced. And before long with that essential aspect of proof still lacking, the idea becomes an accepted fact that "everyone knows."

Before looking at **the major arguments for and against a rotating, orbiting earth,** two important issues must be noted which are "weighted to influence the outcome". The conditioning process toward heliocentricity is dependent upon the denial of the ether and creative mathematics.

Creative Mathematics

It is no new thing to construct an impressive mathematical model for a theory that may be true but no one knows for certain whether it actually is. In the hands of an able theorist mathematics can become a convincing art form. It has been shown that it can be manipulated to "prove" just about any theory it wants to prove.

N. M. Gwynne is far from being alone when he observes:

> …if a thing could be shown to be mathematically true it was true even if common sense showed it to be false.... (Einstein and Modern Physics, p.64).

Herbert Dingle is scathing:

> I think it is impossible to doubt that as a general rule the practice of mathematical physics goes hand in hand with a lack of elementary reasoning power…(Science at the Crossroads, p.127).

As we will see, it was the creative use of mathematics that produced the formulas for the strange notion that when an objects speed increases, it shrinks in the direction of its movement. George Fitzgerald proposed the idea, and Hendrik Lorentz added the mathematics. Why they did this is quite a story!

It was the brilliant mathematician, Johannes Kepler, who was able to provide the equations for the geocentric observations of Tycho Brahe, and after Brahe's death give the same observations, through mathematics, a heliocentric result.

And, it was the towering Newton, who without presenting actual proof, was able to provide the necessary mathematics to make the heliocentric assumptions a "reality."

By this means, for example, he was able to provide the rotating earth with an equatorial bulge! But before looking at this bulge, we need for the sake of perspective to see how fast we are supposed to be travelling.

Earth's Total Supposed Speed

With absolutely no sense of motion, we are told that we are moving, and that at a rapid clip! The 1038 mph figure for earth's "rotation" has been frequently cited. This is very pedestrian and only the beginning for Big Bang cosmology. The following adds the supposed velocity of earth's rotation to its velocity around the sun – to the velocity of the solar system through the galaxy, and finally to the speed of the galaxy through space.

> **69,361 MPH Spin and Orbit**
> **43,200 MPH Towards Lambda Herculis**
> **15,624 MPH Perpendicular to Galactic Plane**
> **446,400 MPH Orbiting the Galactic Center {or Galactic Spin Rate}**
> -------------------
> **574,585 MPH Speed of Earth within Our Galaxy**

So for every hour, the earth is moving more than half a million miles within our galaxy, and in several directions. Now to this we must add **the speed of our galaxy through space which is another 1,339,200 MPH** which when added to the **574,585 MPH = 1,913,785 MPH** or almost **TWO MILLION MPH.**
> (http://www.thelivingmoon.com/41pegasus/02files/Speed_of_Earth.html).

Yet we have absolutely no sense or feeling of this extreme speed! This two million mph multi–directional velocity has no discernible effect on us. Nor does it seem to have any real effect on the 300 mile high atmosphere that that is riding on the "speeding" earth. How can we be so oblivious to it? We will come back to this, but return now to see where "creative mathematics" can lead.

1. Earths Supposed Oblateness (Equatorial Bulge)

In 1672 the great Tychonian astronomer Jean Dominque Cassini sent Jean Richer from Paris to the equatorial island of Cayenne to observe a total eclipse of the sun. While there Richer noted that the period of a pendulum clock calibrated in Paris had lengthened and was losing about two and a half minutes a day. This slower movement of the pendulum on the equator in contrast to that at Paris' latitude was given a ready explanation by Newton 15 years later. He postulated that the centrifugal force of the earth's rotation would cause a flattening of the earth at the poles and a bulge at the equator. With this bulge increasing the distance to the earth's center, it was explained that gravity would be somewhat less at Cayenne than Paris resulting in a slower pendulum period. We would like to know, however, whether this clock phenomenon was tested at other locations.

More specifically mathpages says:

> According to Newtonian mechanics the spinning of a planet on its axis should cause it to bulge at the equator. This is the content of Proposition 18 of Book III of the Principia, and in Proposition 19 Newton estimates that the equatorial diameter of the Earth differs from the polar diameter by about 1 part in 230. (Modern estimates are about 1 part in 297.4.). One of the confirmations of Newton's theory was provided by the astronomer Giovanni Domenico Cassini, director of the Paris observatory, who determined by direct observation that the planet Jupiter is (as Newton's theory predicts) wider at its equator than from pole to pole. (*The Bulging Earth*,
> http://www.mathpages.com/home/kmath182/kmath182.htm)

Note that the idea of a bulging earth began with mathematics! And, mathematics that was based on the unproven assumption that the earth spins. Note that this was followed by an argument from analogy, Jupiter spins and becomes oblate, so must the earth. But remember, Jupiter is a gas giant. Science believes that earth developed its bulge early in its evolution when it was malleable. As mathpage says: "the entire Earth was once spinning in a molten state, so we would expect it to have solidified with an equatorial bulge". When the Biblical creationist accepts heliocentric arguments he must consider the implications. When does the creationist say the earth was malleable enough to develop a bulge?

Note further that the current estimate of earth's oblateness is considerably less than that proposed by Newton. And, according to mathpage, the current figure is an estimate. As to how a bulge of 1 part in 297.4 would translate, we are told:

> The Earth has an equatorial bulge of 42.72 km (26.5 miles) due to its rotation: its diameter measured across the equatorial plane (12756.28 km, 7,927 miles) is 42.72 km more than that measured between the poles (12713.56 km, 7,900 miles). To identify the Earth's radius, these numbers must be divided by two. I.e, anyone on either pole may be 21.36 km

closer to the earth's centrepoint than if standing on the equator. ("Equatorial bulge," Wikipedia).

In fact 26.5 miles divided into the equatorial diameter of 7,927 miles would be a little over 1 part in 299. This means that the equator is elevated about 13.25 miles higher than the poles from earth's center. What implications would this have for a long south flowing river like the Mississippi? One wonders also if the lowering of this estimate is going to continue!

With Newton as the basis, modern physic's explanation of the earth's oblatness is far more complex, confusing and contradictory than we have thus far mentioned. We are told that it is the mass of the universe (called in this context the inertial frame of reference) that pulls the spinning earth out of shape. And that earth's centrifugal force is only a fictitious force! "It does not really exist; it is simply an apparent effect due to circular motion." (Philip Stott, "The Earth's Position and Motions," The Earth Our Home, p. 21).

Gerardus Bouw explains further:

> Newton did offer a proof for what he termed absolute space [the fixed star shell, being nearly at rest in reference to the rotating earth]. Imagine a cup of water. The surface of the water will be flat. Now stir the water. As the water circles faster and faster in the cup, its surface becomes more and more concave. Since the water is rotating with respect to its surroundings, namely, the universe, Newton concluded that the surroundings provided an absolute, immovable space. Today such is called an inertial frame of reference. The force which distorted the surface of the water is called the centrifugal force. Interestingly, according to modern physics centrifugal force is not a real force but it is regarded as a fictitious force

> and is thus properly termed the centrifugal effect? By contrast, in the geocentric universe the centrifugal effect is a real, gravitational force….

> The usual claim is that the universe provides an inertial frame of reference. What that means is that the mass of the universe establishes a force (gravitational field) which affects bodies within it. Thus the inertial field of the universe is said to pull the earth out of shape so that it has a bulge at the equator. (*Geocentricity*, pp. 225, 226).

This is quite an admission! Modern physics tells us that phenomena such as the Coriolis effect and Foucault pendulum movement is due to the earth's rotation; here though Newtonian physics states that the mass of the universe can have a causal effect upon the earth. The geocentricist accepts this, but with a "role reversal" difference: It is what heliocentricists call the inertial frame of reference that is moving not the earth!

Regarding the supposed difference in gravity on the equator in contrast to the poles we are told:

> Because of a planet's rotation around its own axis, the gravitational acceleration is less at the equator than at the poles…. Measurements of the acceleration due to gravity at the equator must also take into account the planet's rotation. Any object that is stationary with

respect to the surface of the Earth is actually following a circular trajectory, circumnavigating the Earth's axis. Pulling an object into such a circular trajectory requires a force. The acceleration that is required to circumnavigate the Earth's axis along the equator at one revolution per sidereal day is 0.0339 m/s². Providing this acceleration decreases the effective gravitational acceleration. At the equator, the effective gravitational acceleration is 9.7805 m/s². This means that the true gravitational acceleration at the equator must be 9.8144 m/s² (9.7805 + 0.0339 = 9.8144).

At the poles, the gravitational acceleration is 9.8322 m/s². The difference of 0.0178 m/s² between the gravitational acceleration at the poles and the true gravitational acceleration at the equator is because objects located on the equator are about 21 kilometers further away from the center of mass of the Earth than at the poles, which corresponds to a smaller gravitational acceleration.

In summary, there are two contributions to the fact that the effective gravitational acceleration is less strong at the equator than at the poles. About 70 percent of the difference is contributed by the fact that objects circumnavigate the Earth's axis, and about 30 percent is due to the non-spherical shape of the Earth. ("Equatorial bulge" *Wikipedia*).

But again it must be stressed that these figures are mathematical and based on the assumption of the earth's rotation, they are not derived by actual measurement.

An Earth ellipsoid is a mathematical figure approximating the shape of the Earth, used as a reference frame for computations in geodesy, astronomy and the geosciences. Various different ellipsoids have been used as approximations. It is an ellipsoid of rotation, whose short (polar) axis (connecting the two flattest spots called geographical north and south poles) is approximately aligned with the rotation axis of the Earth. ("Earth ellipsoid" *Wikipedia*, emphasis mine).

Again it is right to ask whether there is any actual measurement involved in these figures or whether it is solely mathematics based on the assumption of a rotating earth.

Satellites and the Oblateness Factor

The calculation of a satellite's orbit assumes and factors in the Newtonian oblateness equations. The resultant "force" is said to be a primary cause of satellite perturbation (deviation).

One of the largest deviations from a perfectly elliptical orbit occurs at a frquency of twice-per-revolution, due to the oblateness term. (Lee-Lang Fu and Anny Cazenave, *Satellite Altimetry and Earth Sciences*, p.68).

Notably the authors say it is one of the largest but not the only significant cause of a satellite's perturbations.

The earth's gravity field is however not perfectly spherical, and undulations in the gravity field corresponding to the variations in the earth's shape and density cause perturbations from perfectly elliptical motion. (p. 67).

It is further stated that if oblateness were ignored, the satellites position would "over a long period of time" be lost.

For example, ignoring the effect of the oblateness of the Earth on an artificial satellite would cause to completely fail in the prediction of its position over a long period of time. (Muhammad Adan, Radzuan Razali and Muhammad Said, *A Study of Perturbation Effect on Satellite Orbit Using Cowell's Method*, p. 1).

As the following shows, there is a contradictory explanation for the effect that oblateness has on a satellite orbiting above the equator. In theory it is stated that it should have no effect; yet as will be see, in practice earth's oblateness is said to have an effect.

It is evident that if the satellite's orbit coincides with the plane of the planet's equator, there will be no force tending to pull it up or down from that plane. In this case, then, there is no disturbance of latitude. (*Penny Cyclopaedia of the Society for the Diffusion of Useful Knowledge*, p. 399).

That is the theory, but as the following shows it is not the practice.

A geostationary orbit is a special case of a geosynchronous orbit. Put the satellite in a very nearly circular orbit (no eccentricity) and give it zero inclination and the satellite will stay over the same point of the earth's equator – in other words, appear to be stationary in the sky. This is the ideal condition for a communications satellite. One would simply point their ground antenna to the spot in the sky where the satellite appears. Unfortunately, orbits are easily perturbed through natural causes, and a geostationary satellite soon drifts from the position and must be forced back to position by firing thrusters.

All geostationary satellites must be located along the celestial equator as viewed from the earth. An international commission "assigns" who gets to put a satellite on a particular longitudinal subpoint. Interestingly, a perturbation caused by the Earth's oblateness, causes a longitudinal acceleration of a satellite in geostationary orbit. The acceleration is zero at 75 degrees east longitude (over the Indian Ocean) and 255 degrees east longitude (over the eastern Pacific Ocean). The lucky owners of these slots get to put their satellites where they are least likely to need fuel to maintain position! All other satellites must use fuel to retain their positions, or they will drift toward these two stable longitudinal points!
(http://www.satobs.org/faq/Chapter-04.txt , emphasis mine).

Therefore except for these two small "parking slots" over the equator where obateness forces should not be a factor, they are in fact said to be factor and the cause of this drift. It is indeed difficult to see how an "oblateness force" could affect a satellite that was on an equatorial plane. This raises the obvious question as to whether this force has been properly accounted for and defined.

Further, while much is made of the effect of the oblateness force upon a satellite, very little can be said of its effect on earth where its effect should be hugely greater. Relying upon mathematics rather than the actual weighing of an object, we are told:

> Taking into account both of the above effects [obateness and centrifugal force]....you weigh about 0.5% more at the poles than at the equator [0.2% for oblateness alone]. (http://curious.astro.cornell.edu/question.php?number=310).

It is difficult to see how two tenths of a percent gravitational difference on earth's surface could have any measurable effect upon a satellite's orbit. And, especially so if this 0.2% is not actually measured but only arrived at mathematically via the assumption of oblateness due to a spinning earth. A search of the Net will show that this figure is always based on mathematical calculation with no example given that the difference was actually weighed.

The credibility of this "oblateness factor" is stretched further when we consider that the above example of "a perturbation caused by the Earth's oblateness" is for a geostationary satellite that is placed on the equatorial plane 22,240 miles above the equator.

To add to our confusion, satellites may in fact be indicating something different than "standard" oblateness.

> The possibility that the Earth's equator is an ellipse rather than a circle and therefore that the ellipsoid is triaxial has been a matter of scientific controversy for many years. Modern technological developments have furnished new and rapid methods for data collection and since the launch of Sputnik 1, orbital data have been used to investigate the theory of ellipticity.
>
> A second theory, more complicated than triaxiality, proposed that observed long periodic orbital variations of the first Earth satellites indicate an additional depression at the south pole accompanied by a bulge of the same degree at the north pole. It is also contended that the northern middle latitudes were slightly flattened and the southern middle latitudes bulged in a similar amount. This concept suggested a slightly pear-shaped Earth and was the subject of much public discussion. Modern geodesy tends to retain the ellipsoid of revolution and treat triaxiality and pear shape as a part of the geoid figure. ("Figure of the Earth" *Wikipedia*).

A 2005 NASA report stated:

> The researchers found over the past 28 years, two large variations in the Earth's oblateness were connected to strong ENSO [El Nino Southern Oscillation] events. Variations in mass distribution, which caused the change in the gravity field, were predominantly over the continents, with a smaller contribution due to changes over the ocean. The cause of a variation in the Earth's mass over the 21-year period between 1978 and 2001, however, still remains a mystery.

Cheng and Tapley's research relied on NASA's SLR data to measure changes in the longest wavelengths of the Earth's gravity field in order to see how the global-scale mass was redistributed around the world.

The Earth's gravity is an invisible force of attraction that pulls masses together. The relative motion of a small lighter object, such as a spacecraft, to a large heavy object such as the Earth, depends on how much mass each object has and how that mass is distributed. Scientists can measure the changes in Earth's gravitational pull using instruments on the ground to track satellites in space. So, water mass shifts on Earth and the changes in shape of the Earth can be detected.
(http://www.nasa.gov/centers/goddard/earthandsun/earthshape.html,) [emphasis mine.]

Since September 2009, the GOCE (Gravity field and Ocean Circulation Explorer) satellite has been on a gravity-mapping orbit over the entire Earth. Flying at the edge of Earth's atmosphere at an altitude of 254.9 km – the lowest orbit that can be sustained over a long period by any Earth observation satellite – the satellite is able to measure differences using three pairs of highly accurate gradiometers.

With the darker red representing stonger gravity forces and the blue weaker, the following gives an initial representation of the Gravity Map. Note the orbital paths.

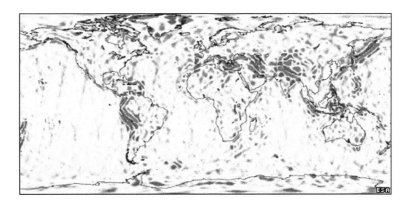

A BBC report explains:

The red colours indicate a positive variation in gravity moving from one place to another - i.e. places where Earth's tug becomes greater. The blue colours indicate a negative variation in gravity - places where Earth's tug is a little less. Simply put, if you were to take some bathroom scales to these locations you would weigh fractionally more in red places and weigh less in blue ones.
(http://news.bbc.co.uk/1/hi/sci/tech/8408957.stm).

In June 2010 the European Space Agency (ESA) released a further map. While the overall conclusion conveyed by the picture is about the same, the explanation given is not so clear.

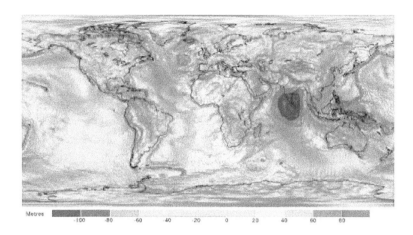

Somewhat confusingly we are told-

> Technically speaking the map shows the Earth's 'geoid' - or which parts of our planet have a greater gravitational pull than other parts because of the different rocks it's made of.

> Stronger gravitational pull is depicted by red, while a weaker pull is depicted by blue.

> If you turned this map into a globe, it would look like a partially blown-up football, where peaks represent strong gravity and the troughs show slightly weaker gravity. If you placed a much smaller ball anywhere on this squashy football, it wouldn't move – even if it was on a slope – because gravity would be exactly the same all over it.
> (http://planetearth.nerc.ac.uk/news/story.aspx?id=763).

Nevertheless, these two gravity maps depict something that is a great deal different than Newtonian oblateness! Based on Newton's equations for a spinning earth the maps should show latitudinal points of deep blue across the equatorial regional and then a gradual change toward deep red at the poles. Unless we are color blind they do not!

Noting that these pictures come from the GOCE satellite (Gravity field and Ocean Circulation Explorer), it is interesting to see that the "oblateness factor" is <u>not</u> used in sea navigation.

> For the purposes of navigation, we assume that we are working with a perfect sphere. The differences between the two diameters are small enough to be considered insignificant. Nautical charts do NOT take Earth's oblateness into account.
> (http://www.tpub.com/content/administration/14220/css/14220_24.htm).

Has Oblateness Been Photographed From Space?

Could a 26.5-mile bulge at the equator be observed from space? You would certainly think so, and this would settle the question. Below is NASA's most popular earth-from-space picture. It shows both poles, a feature that is difficult to find on the Net. Though enhanced, it likely gives an accurate picture of earth as a sphere. Compare the circle of the earth in Isaiah 40:22.

This true-color image shows North and South America as they would appear from space 35,000 km (22,000 miles) above the Earth. The image is a combination of data from two satellites. The Moderate Resolution Imaging Spectroradiometer (MODIS) instrument aboard NASA's Terra satellite collected the land surface data over 16 days, while NOAA's Geostationary Operational Environmental Satellite (GOES) produced a snapshot of the Earth's clouds (NASA Earth Observatory).

Earth from 22,000 Miles

If the image is enlarged sufficiently the 26.5-mile oblateness across the equator should be measurable. Marshall Hall estimates that if the picture were enlarged to just under nine feet, a bulge of 3/8 of an inch should be detected on the equator (The Earth is not Moving, p. 197). This should not be too difficult, but a search of the Web has not yielded an example of specific photographic measurements. Some do say it can or has been done, but specific examples have not been found.

> Earth's actual shape, however, is so close to being a perfect sphere that the eye cannot detect its oblateness. When viewed from space, Earth appears perfectly round, lets suppose that we made a scale model of the Earth – a globe. If we used a scale of 1 centimeter = 1,000 kilometres, the globe would have a polar diameter of 12.714 centimeter and an equatorial diameter of 12.756 centimeters – a little bigger than a softball. The difference in diameters would be 0.042 centimeter, or less than half a millimeter! We would need a micrometer to measure the difference in diameters (Denecke, Edward J, Jr., Carr, William H. *Lets Review: Earth Science*, 2006, p. 67).

If the matter is going to be discussed and earth actually does have a 26.5 mile bulge, this should be pursued further than giving the measurements of a soft ball! And again:

Most obviously, pictures taken from space provide evidence of the Earth's shape. The Earth is so close to being a perfect sphere that when viewed from any point in space the Earth appears spherical. If accurate measurements are performed, however, it can be shown that the Earth is not quite a perfect circle.
(http://www.regentsprep.org/regents/earthsci/units/introduction/oblate.cfm).

If this is so, details of such photographic measurements should be readily accessible on the Net. To say, "If accurate measurements are performed", is not the same as saying they have been performed. Perhaps others may find something. But a search of the Net has not yielded a specific example where photographs were measured to show earth's obateness.

Does The Mississippi Flow Uphill?

When the equator (measuring the radius from earth's center) is elevated 13.25 miles higher than the poles, a number of anomalies appear. An often-cited example is that the peak of Mount Chimborazo in Ecuador, rather than Mount Everest, becomes the highest point on earth. The explanation given is that: "Since the oceans, like the earth and the atmosphere, also bulge, Chimborazo is not as high above sea level as Everest." But is that explanation valid? Would we not rather expect the oceans to fiind their lowest level with reference to <u>earth's center of mass</u> regardless of the oblateness factor at the surface? Certainly an appeal cannot be made to earth's rotation as the force drawing such a huge amount of water to the equatorial region. As shown above, that force is not nearly strong enough.

What implications does this have for a long south-flowing river like the Mississippi? With the earth's center as the reference point, it means simply that this great river is in fact flowing uphill before emptying into the Gulf of Mexico?

The Traveler's Journal describes the Mississippi's <u>three-mile uphill flow</u>.

> Earth's equatorial bulge gives rise to a host of other geographic oddities. For example, New Orleans, which is located at about 29 degrees north latitude, happens to be nearly three miles farther from the earth's center than Lake Itasca, Minn., headwaters of the Mississippi River, which is situated a shade under 47 degrees north latitude. Thus, Old Man River is forced to flow uphill on its 2,340-mile journey to the Gulf of Mexico.
> (http://www.travelersjournal.com/articles2.php?ID=291).

And further, what would keep the Gulf from flowing back up (or is it down) the Mississippi? And, for that matter, what keeps the oceans from flooding back toward the poles? What began with Newton writing a simple formula for the rotation of earth can certainly bring the idea of an oblate earth into some deep waters.

Having mentioned satellites we now come to the most remarkable and curious of the different kinds of satellites.

2. The Geostationary Satellite

Man-made satellites may be either LEO (Low Earth Orbit), MEO (Mid Earth Orbit) or Geosynchronous Geostationary. The first two are seen orbiting the earth; but the Geosynchronous/Geostationary satellite appears to be "parked" motionless at a very much higher altitude over the earth. The LEO satellites orbit at between 200-400 miles, and include the space shuttles and the international space station. These orbit at between 173-286 miles and thereby keep exposure to the radiation of the Van Allen Belts at a tolerable minimum. The MEOs orbit once every twelve hours, and at an altitude of about 12,000 miles. These comprise the satellites of the Global Positioning System and track planes, ships, cars etc.

In contrast to all the other satellites that are actually seen orbiting above the surface of the earth, our interest here is with the Geosynchronous/Geostationary type which because their orbit is said to be synchronized exactly with the earth's rotation do not appear to move (or move only slightly). In this they bear directly on the question of whether or not the earth is spinning. Regarding the two names given to these satellites, geosynchronous and geostationary, though commonly used interchangeably, there is a distinction.

> If a geosynchronous satellite's orbit is not exactly aligned with the Earth's equator, the orbit is called an inclined orbit. It will appear (when viewed by someone on the ground) to oscillate daily around a fixed point. As the angle between the orbit and the equator decreases, the magnitude of this oscillation becomes smaller; when the orbit lies entirely over the equator, assuming a circular orbit, the satellite remains stationary relative to the Earth's surface – it is said to be geostationary ("Geosynchronous Satellite", *Wikipedia*).

When the terms are used precisely, the satellites are called geostationary (GSO) when:

- Their orbit is said to be circular, and synchronous with the rotation of the earth.
- Their orbit is at a constant altitude of 22,236 miles above sea level.
- They remain stationary over a fixed point on the equator.

They are called geosynchronous (GEO) when:

- Their orbit is elliptical, and synchronous with the rotation of the earth.
- Their orbital altitude varies.
- They move in an analemma (a figure-eight oscillation) over a fixed point at   latitudes above or below the equatorial plane.

Consider this further explanation, and note the effect of other stellar bodies on the satellite:

> A geostationary orbit occurs when an object (satellite) is placed approximately 37,000 km (23,000 mi) above the Earth's equator with the characteristic that, from a fixed observation point on the Earth's surface, it appears motionless. A satellite is in an inclined orbit when its orbital plane is tipped some number of degrees from the horizontal defined by the equator. In the case of an inclined geosynchronous orbit, although the satellite remains geosynchronous (that is, completing one orbit around the earth every 24 hours), it is no

longer geostationary. From a fixed observation point on Earth, it would appear to trace out a small ellipse as <u>the gravitational effects of other stellar bodies (Sun & Moon) exhibit influence over the satellite</u>, as the effect accumulates over time the trace becomes an

analemma with lobes oriented north-southward. The satellite traces the same analemma once each sidereal day.

A geostationary orbit is not stable. It takes regular manoeuvres to actively counteract the above gravitational forces. The majority of the fuel of the satellite, typically hydrazine is spent for this purpose. Otherwise, the satellite experiences a change in the inclination over time. At the end of the satellite's lifetime, when fuel approaches depletion, satellite operators may decide to omit these expensive manoeuvres to correct inclination and only control eccentricity [elongation of the circular orbit]. This prolongs the life-time of the satellite as it consumes less fuel over time, but the satellite can then only be used by ground antennae capable of following the north-south movement, Satellite Tracking earth stations. Before the fuel comes to an end, satellites can be moved to a graveyard orbit to keep the geostationary altitude free for subsequent missions ("Inclined Orbit," *Wikipedia,* emphasis mine).

Our interest here is with the Geostationary rather than the Geosynchronous Satellite, and especially as we believe this term describes the true nature of the case. If it is truly stationary then the earth cannot be rotating.

These fixed satellites are used in global communications. They provide TV images of the weather patterns and clouds we see moving across an area. They also send the TV signals received by home satellite dishes. These dishes and other ground-based antennas do not need to track them, but remain aimed in one fixed direction. In considering these millions of permanently aimed antennas and dishes over the world, we are immediately struck with how precisely accurate the maintenance of the satellites position must be in order for the signal to be received. If it is out even slightly it will not work. This brings us to a very basic question.

Which of these two possibilities is the more likely explanation of how these Geostationary Satellites work?

1. At an altitude of 22,236 miles the satellite is kept aloft by its *orbital velocity*. The *rapidly moving* satellite is then synchronized and adjusted to maintain an exact position over the same spot on the *spinning* earth.

2. At an altitude of 22,236 miles the satellite is kept aloft by *equilibrium* between earth's gravity and the pull of a *spinning* universe. The *stationary* satellite is then adjusted to maintain an exact position over the same spot on the *stationary* earth.

A great deal of debate may ensue on whether it is *orbital velocity* or *equilibrium with other stellar bodies* that keeps this kind of satellite aloft. There can be little doubt however that when once it is aloft, which view would present the greater difficulty in lining up a beam to a satellite dish. Both views must provide a fixed beam, but with the first it comes from a speeding satellite to a spinning earth, while in the second, the satellite, the beam and the earth are each fixed. On consideration, the difficulties involved with the first view approach being *insurmountable*!

1. *Consider the altitude*. In comparison with all other satellites, the distance from earth at which Geostationary Satellites operate is huge (22,236 miles). When this distance is compounded with the size of the orbital circumference, the satellite's speed, and the earths spin – an infinitely greater challenge for exact placement is posed then if both the satellite and earth were stationary.

2. *Consider the orbital circumference*. At an altitude of 22,236 miles, the circumference of the satellite's daily orbit around the earth would be 164,560 miles. And, in order for the beam to be received it would have to remain precisely at this circumference.

3. *Consider the satellites speed*. With an orbital circumference of 164,560 miles (divided by 24 hours), the satellite would have to travel at 6,856 mph to keep up with a fixed point on the equatorial plane of the spinning earth. And, it must remain exactly at that speed.

4. *Consider the earth's rotational speed*. A fixed point on the equator is said to travelling at 1038 mph. This must match perfectly with the speeding satellite.

5. *Consider the exact synchronization required*. Multiplied millions of dishes along the earth's different latitudes are locked on to these far distant satellites, and receive perfect signals, day after day, month after month, year after year. The slightest alteration to the required synchronization would make this impossible and soon overwhelm the capabilities of the repositioning thrusters. If for example as claimed there is a slight but frequent fluctuation of the earth's rotational speed, there would have to be a correspondingly exact and continual synchronization of the satellites speed.

6. *Consider the violation of Kepler's elliptical orbits*. We saw in Kepler's laws of elliptical orbital motion that an object in its orbit around the sun or some other center, must "sweep through equal areas in equal times". This means that the object (including man made satellites) is constantly altering its speed and constantly altering its altitude. As it elliptically orbits closest to its center (perigee) it is moving faster, while at its furthest point (apogee) it is moving slower. Such is the case for all satellites except the Geostationary Satellite. For it, such motion would be impossible. It must move in a circular orbit where both velocity and altitude are constant. Why then the exception! Why if it is only orbiting as other satellites except that its orbit synchronizes with the earth's rotation is it required to disobey Kepler's laws? The Geostationary Satellite does not have a perigee and apogee. It stays in the same place. And, we believe this is actual and not apparent.

7. *Consider the satellite's daily "return"*. The satellite must match so precisely the earth's rotation that not only does it remain over a fixed point on the equator, but day after day (sidereal) at the same precise time must return to the same fixed point against the background stars.

On reflection, the difficulties for a spinning earth (1,038 mph) to remain in perfect synchronization with a satellite that travels at an extremely high altitude (22,236 miles), and at a high velocity (6,856 mph), and over an enormous daily circumference (164,560 miles), and yet day after day have these functions and figures remain perfectly constant so that the satellite remains fixed over the same point on the Equator, and daily returns to same point against the background stars, seems to press too far the bounds of probability. And, to multiply this by the many other interconnected satellites doing exactly the same thing, and giving perfect reception to a billion TV receivers….. We conclude therefore that the geostationary satellite strongly argues for a stationary earth.

The more we think about the spinning earth /speeding satellite explanation for the Geostationary Satellite, the more the questions. For example, if we look up at this kind of satellite (fixed in the sky, showing no motion) and consider how it beams directly down to where we are standing (again no sense of motion under foot), we would think that it should be theoretically possible for it to descend directly down to us. This in fact appears to be the case!

3. The Space Elevator

The long proposed Space Elevator is the ultimate Geostationary Satellite, and as such reveals further the true nature and implications of this this kind of satellite. Tethered by a cable from an altitude of 22,236 miles (or more) to a spot on the equator, it brings further into the realm of fantasy the idea of a spinning earth and a satellite orbiting at 6,856 mph.

A January 20, 2009 *London Times* article reports:

> Ever since it was first popularized by Arthur C. Clarke, the idea of a "space elevator" has languished in the realms of science fiction. But now a team of British scientists has taken the first step on what could be a high-tech stairway to heaven.
>
> Spurred on by a $4 million research prize from NASA, a team at Cambridge University has created the world's strongest ribbon: a cylindrical strand of carbon that combines lightweight flexibility with incredible strength and has the potential to stretch vast distances.
>
> The development has been seized upon by the space scientists, who believe the technology could allow astronauts to travel into space via a cable thousands of miles long — a space elevator.
>
> They predict the breakthrough will revolutionize space travel. Such an elevator could potentially offer limitless and cheap space travel.
>
> At a stroke, it would make everything from tourism to more ambitious expeditions to Mars commercially viable. The idea couldn't come too soon for NASA, which spends an estimated $500 million every time the shuttle blasts off, not to mention burning about 900 tons of polluting rocket fuel.

Among several others, a Japanese company has announced that it is pressing ahead with similar plans:

> People could be gliding up to space on high-tech elevators by 2050 if a Japanese construction company's ambitious plans come to fruition. Tokyo-based Obayashi Corp. wants to build an operational space elevator by the middle of the century, Japan's Yomiuri Shimbun newspaper reported Wednesday (Feb. 22, 2012). The device would carry passengers skyward at 124 mph, delivering them to a station 22,000 miles above Earth in a little more than a week.
>
> In Obayashi's vision, a cable would be stretched from a spaceport on Earth's surface up to an altitude of 60,000 miles (96,000 km), or about one-quarter of the distance between our planet and the moon. A counterweight at its end would help "anchor" the cable in space.
>
> A 30-passenger car would travel along the cable, possibly using magnetic linear motors as a means of propulsion, Yomiuri Shimbun reported. Passengers would disembark at the station, which would house living quarters and laboratory space, along with a solar-power generation facility capable of transmitting power to the ground….
>
> One major hurdle has been finding a material strong and light enough to build the incredibly long cable. Obayashi's optimism is fuelled partly by its belief that a suitable material has finally been identified — tiny cylindrical structures called carbon nanotubes, which were first developed in the 1990s. But nanotube tech isn't quite ready yet; engineers likely must find a way to manufacture them more cheaply and efficiently to make space elevators feasible, company officials said.
>
> Indeed, the elevator's price tag could be the steepest hurdle to its construction. "At this moment, we cannot estimate the cost for the project," an Obayashi official said, according to Yomiuri Shimbun. "However, we'll try to make steady progress so that it won't end just up as simply a dream."
>
> Obayashi is not the only entity taking this dream seriously. For example, NASA researchers released a lengthy report more than a decade ago citing the potential of carbon nanotubes to make space elevators possible. And the agency has sponsored the Space Elevator Games, a contest to develop precursors to this longed-for transportation system.
> (http://www.space.com/14656-japanese-space-elevator-2050-proposal.html)

This may sound fanciful, and in some cases there may be a "hint of publicity," but it has been a subject of serious scientific inquiry for over a century, and the basic concept despite huge logistical problems is considered possible. The one primary reason why it is considered to be in with a chance is because of that remarkable phenomenon already mentioned.

The Special Altitude

Whether a Geostationary Satellite is kept aloft by orbital velocity and maintains an exact spot over a spinning earth, or whether it stays aloft and maintains the same spot by equilibrium between earth's gravity and the pull of a spinning universe, one thing will be the same: this keeping aloft must be at an altitude of 22,236 miles above sea level.

The conventional "explanation" for the so called *magic altitude* is as follows:

> According to Kepler's Third Law, the orbital period of a satellite in a circular orbit increases with increasing altitude. Space stations and Shuttles in Low Earth orbit (LEO), typically two to four hundred miles above the Earth's surface, make between fifteen and sixteen revolutions per day. The Moon, at an altitude of about 238,900 miles, takes about 27 days 7 hours to make a complete revolution. Between those extremes lies the **"magic" altitude** of 22,236 miles at which a satellite's orbital period matches the period at which the Earth rotates: once every sidereal day (23 hours 56 minutes 4 seconds). In that case, the satellite is said to be geosynchronous ("Geosynchronous Satellite," *Wikipedia*).

But why does the satellite's orbital period (its daily orbit of the earth) match the daily rotation of the earth when it is at an altitude of 22, 236 miles? And, why does that make a difference? Like Newton's laws for gravity, this is a statement of what happens, not why it happens.

This explanation is flawed, because Kepler's Three Laws deal with elliptical rather than circular orbits. His First Law states that bodies move in an elliptical orbit, and this means their velocity varies constantly. His Third Law is based on this principle. The examples given in the explanation do not use circular orbits. The one exception (WHY?) is the supposed orbit (circular!) of the Geostationary Satellite.

Notwithstanding the inability of science to explain this crucial altitude, 23,236 will be the top floor (or just above) for the Space Elevator.

"All Aboard"!

Our senses tell us that if we look up at a satellite that appears to be stationary, and we ourselves by all accounts are stationary, then in theory we should both be standing still and should be able to travel directly to each other. Though certainly not by intention, the Space Elevator demonstrates this principle. It gives an insight into the actual nature of the Geostationary Satellite, and becomes a compelling indicator that both the satellite and the the earth are standing still.

Initially the idea for the Space Elevator was to build from the ground up. Again, consider the implications: Would we prefer a swinging 22,238 mile high tower, or one that is stable and motionless? Which is the more likely?

> The key concept of the space elevator appeared in 1895 when Russian scientist Konstantin Tsiolkovsky was inspired by the Eiffel Tower in Paris to consider a tower that reached all the way into space, built from the ground up to the altitude of geostationary orbit (22,238 mi) above sea level. He noted that a "celestial castle" at the top of such a spindle-shaped cable would have the "castle" orbiting Earth in a geostationary orbit (i.e. the castle would remain over the same spot on Earth's surface).

Since the elevator would attain orbital velocity (6,856 mph) as it rode up the cable, an object released at the tower's top would also have the orbital velocity necessary to remain

in geostationary orbit. Unlike more recent concepts for space elevators, Tsiolkovsky's tower was a compression structure, rather than a tension (or "tether") structure.

Building a compression structure from the ground up proved an unrealistic task as there was no material in existence with enough compressive strength to support its own weight

under such conditions. In 1959 another Russian scientist, Yuri N. Artsutanov, suggested a more feasible proposal. Artsutanov suggested using a geostationary satellite as the base from which to deploy the structure downward. By using a counterweight, a cable would be lowered from geostationary orbit to the surface of Earth, while the counterweight was extended from the satellite away from Earth, keeping the cable constantly over the same spot on the surface of the Earth. Artsutanov's idea was introduced to the Russian-speaking public in 1960. ("Space Elevator," *Wikipedia* with sources)

Space Elevator

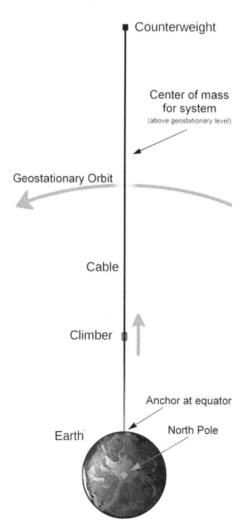

The Space Elevator

With this illustration, we look down upon the earth from above the North Pole, and view the earth's supposed rotation in an easterly direction (right to left). Our senses, however, tell us that the sun is moving west (to the right). The following from a heliocentric perspective explains how the Space Elevator will work.

> A space elevator for Earth would consist of a cable fixed to the Earth's equator, reaching into space. By attaching a counterweight at the end (or by further extending the cable upward for the same purpose), the center of mass is kept well above the level of geostationary orbit. Upward centrifugal force from the Earth's rotation ensures that the cable remains stretched taut, fully countering the downward gravitational pull. Once above the geostationary level, climbers would have weight in the upward direction as the centrifugal force overpowers gravity.

Yes, in theory it is possible, but of the two perspectives this is going to be the one that is difficult! It is far easier to envisage the spinning universe providing the upward pull on the horizontally stationary elevator rising from the stationary earth. Again consider the explanation as to how the elevator will lift off from a spinning earth, and at geostationary height reach an orbital velocity of over six times that of the earth's rotation.

> A space elevator cable rotates along with the rotation of the Earth. Objects fastened to the cable will experience upward centrifugal force that opposes some of, all of, or more than, the downward gravitational force at that point. The higher up the cable, the stronger is the upward centrifugal force and the more it opposes the downward gravity. Eventually it becomes stronger than gravity above the geosynchronous level.

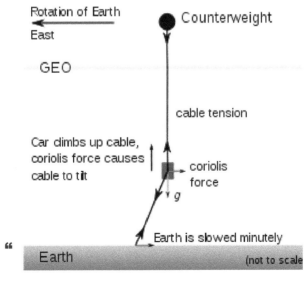

How It Works"

As the car climbs, the elevator takes on a 1 degree lean, due to the top of the elevator traveling faster than the bottom around the Earth (Coriolis force). [Note: the Coriolis force we experience would be much more violent if the earth was truly spinning].

The horizontal speed of each part of the cable increases with altitude, proportional to distance from the center of the Earth, reaching orbital velocity at a point 66% of the height between the surface and geostationary orbit [This 66% is explained below]. As a payload is lifted up on the cable, it gains not only altitude, but horizontal speed (angular momentum) as well. This angular momentum is taken from the Earth's own rotation. As the climber ascends, it is initially moving slightly more slowly than each successive part of cable it is moving on to. This is the Coriolis force, the climber "drags" (Westward) on the cable as it climbs.

The overall effect of the centrifugal force acting on the cable causes it to constantly try to return to the energetically favourable vertical orientation, so after an object has been lifted on the cable the counterweight will swing back towards the vertical like an inverted pendulum. Space elevators and their loads will be designed so that the center of mass is always well-enough above the level of geostationary orbit to hold up the whole system. Lift and descent operations must be carefully planned so as to keep the pendulum-like motion of the counterweight around the tether point under control. When the payload has reached a level greater than 66% of the distance from the surface to GEO, the horizontal speed is enough that the payload would enter an orbit if released from the cable.

The opposite process would occur for payloads descending the elevator, tilting the cable eastwards and insignificantly increasing Earth's rotation speed. It has also been proposed to use a second cable attached to a platform to lift payload up the main cable, since the lifting device would not have to deal with its own weight against Earth's gravity.

The means of powering the lifting device continues to present a challenge. Another design constraint will be the ascending speed of the climber. As geosynchronous orbit is at (22,236 mi), assuming the climber can reach the speed of 180 mph it will take 5 days to climb to geosynchronous orbit. Design of the counter weight above geostationary orbit also presents a big challenge. ("Space Elevator" Wikipedia)

Thus, we are being asked to believe that from the spinning earth, the Space Elevator will swing from a 22,236+ mile tether, at a velocity more than six times (6,856 mph) that of the earth's rotation. This could be quite a ride!

Nevertheless, the fact that such a project is being seriously considered, points (if unintentionally) to the true nature of the case: Neither the Geostationary Satellite nor the Earth over which it is parked is moving.

4. The Atmosphere: Impossible on a Speeding Earth

In presenting the Biblical and Observational Case for Geocentricity, we note first a   number of the Biblical statements concerning the atmosphere:

> *When I made the cloud the garment thereof for the earth, and thick darkness a swaddlingband for it* (Job 38:9).

> *The wind goeth toward the south, and turneth about unto the north; it whirleth about continually, and the wind returneth again according to his circuits* (Eccl. 1:6).

> *He causeth the vapours to ascend from the ends of the earth; he maketh lightnings for the rain; he bringeth the wind out of his treasuries* (Psalms 135:7).

> *When he uttereth his voice, there is a multitude of waters in the heavens, and he causeth the vapours to ascend from the ends of the earth; he maketh lightnings with rain, and bringeth forth the wind out of his treasures* (Jer. 10:13; repeated in 51:16).

> *For, lo, he that formeth the mountains, and createth the wind…(Amos 4:13).*

> *But the men marvelled, saying, What manner of man is this, that even the winds and the sea obey him!* (Matt. 8:27).

> *While the earth remaineth, seedtime and harvest, and cold and heat, and summer and winter, and day and night shall not cease* (Gen. 8:22. See also Job 28:23-27; Job 38:17; Psalms 107:25; 147:17,18; 148:8; Prov. 30:4).

God created the atmosphere with its circuits, clouds, weather patterns, and yearly cycles: all maintained by His power, yet now all disordered and under the curse through the fall of Adam.

> *For we know that the whole creation groaneth and travaileth in pain together until now* (Rom. 8:22).

Therefore, whatever secondary means may be employed by the Lord, when we consider the atmosphere with its weather patterns and winds, we look to Him as the Prime Mover. The Bible clearly addresses the movements of earth's weather systems, but it never speaks of the earth moving (except in times of judgement).

Regarding the Observational Case, the atmosphere, the weather, the air around us must certainly give a "ready at hand" indication as to whether or not the earth is moving.

We are told the earth is speeding through space at a multi-directional two million mph, yet we have absolutely no sense or feeling of this extreme speed! We "know" this because we are told so. But how can the Bible and our own senses be so silent and unaware of this? Therefore, it will be interesting to see what indication the atmosphere with its weather systems give to this question. Does it give the slightest hint that it is riding on an earth at these hyper-speeds? The answer is NO! Does it give any indication that it is travelling on an eastward spinning earth? The answer is the OPPOSITE of what we would expect. While the winds move in all directions, the jet streams move east, and weather systems also generally move east. On an eastward spinning earth we would expect them to move west.

Adding to this anomaly, AMDG succinctly blogs:

> The greatest winds should be at the equator…… this area is actually the opposite – the doldrums. Ooops.
> Eastward rotation should produce westward winds – wrong again, jet streams are eastward…
> (http://scienceblogs.com/startswithabang/2010/09/13/geocentrism-was-galileo-wrong/
> Sept. 14, 2010)

Some good questions are in order:

Why is the Atmosphere Not "Flung Off"?

This was the question that asked both before and after Copernicus, and an argument against his theory. Would not the atmosphere simply be left behind? Would not its fate be similar to that as seen in the tail of a comet? How can the atmosphere move naturally: in different directions, up and down, in periodic circuits maintaining the earth's weather balance, and yet all the while beneath it is an earth travelling two million mph? Surely at some stage common sense must prevail!

Again, if such speeds are in fact a reality, why does not the earth's atmosphere behave at least to some extent like Halley's Comet? Remember we are talking about a comet – that passes through space, not a meteor – that passes through earth's atmosphere.

Halley's Comet

Notice how a Big Bang cosmologist deals with the following question: "So we've got this giant wet rock hurtling through space at incredibly high speeds. It spins, and it revolves around the Sun. Why, with all of this, do we still have something as tenuous as our atmosphere?"

1. The Earth is moving really fast. Just like Galileo said. How fast? Each year, the Earth travels 584 million miles to go around the Sun, for a mean speed of about 67,000 miles per hour. But unlike objects on Earth that move that quickly, there's no drag force in space. Since space is so empty, there's nothing to burn the atmosphere off the way that meteors burn up when they get too close to the Earth. So instead the Earth, which moves at the same speed as its atmosphere, can keep its atmosphere intact simply through the force of its gravity.

2. The Earth is spinning quickly. So why doesn't the atmosphere get flung off of the planet? Although the Earth rotates very fast, once a day, that only gives the surface of the Earth moving at a pathetic 1000 miles-per-hour. Sounds fast, but it isn't a problem for two reasons. First off, just like a centrifuge, spinning things (like the Earth) tend to throw off things on their surface (like the atmosphere). But the Earth's gravity is about 300 times stronger than this centrifugal force, so the atmosphere is fine. Second, even though the Earth is spinning, the atmosphere spins with the Earth, due to the law of conservation of angular momentum. So again, our atmosphere is fine.

3. But objects like Comets lose everything when they orbit the Sun! Why doesn't the Earth lose its atmosphere the same way? Although the Sun's light does hit the Earth's atmosphere, giving individual atoms and molecules tremendous amounts of energy, the energy from the Sun just isn't enough at this great distance to overcome Earth's gravity. The atoms in the atmosphere still stay bound to the planet. For comets, they're tiny, and their gravity is tiny, so they leave a wake of debris (comet tails) through space. But the Earth is big enough, it's gravity is strong enough, and so its atmosphere stays right here with us on our journey forward in space and time. (http://startswithabang.com/?p=1141).

This answer says gravity will keep the atmosphere intact for earth's rotational and orbital velocities (about 69,361 mph). That is doubtful, but granting the possibility, it is only the beginning! There is silence as to how gravity will cope with the atmosphere on an earth hurtling through space at nearly TWO MILLION MPH.

Further, a response cannot be allowed that refers to earth's rotational speed as a "pathetic 1000 miles-per-hour," when according to their cosmology this is sufficient to cause a bulge at the equator. They cannot have it both ways!

Or better yet, as one has asked, if "the atmosphere is magically velcroed to the Earth and constantly rotates from West to East along with it, then … "

- How is it that clouds, wind and weather patterns often travel in opposing   directions simultaneously?

- Why don't East to West traveling planes or projectiles encounter increased resistance?

- Why can I feel the slightest Westward breeze but not the Earth's supposed 1,000 mph Eastward spin?

- If gravitational force is so great to pull the atmosphere together with the Earth then how come little birds and bugs are able to fly?
http://iamtymaximus.wordpress.com/2012/05/08/the-geocentricity-vs-heliocentricity-arguments-side-by-side-then-you-decide-part-two/

Why Does the Atmosphere Not Move Strongly to the West?

Leaving these heightened speeds, let us concentrate only upon earth's supposed west to east spin of 1038 mph.

> The claim that the …atmosphere spins at the same speed as earth is an empty claim. They cannot demonstrate this with a model because gas does not have the same inertia as a solid (http://www.youtube.com/watch?v=xokMcO3T0SY).

That is, a gas cannot, even with gravity, retain the same motions of the solid upon which it rests. Therefore with earth's easterly rotation, there should be a prevailing westerly drift of the atmosphere. Even if weather systems move in all directions, there should still be an overall and decisive movement to the west. If the earth's easterly rotation is a major factor in wind and atmospheric patterns; if it is the cause of the Coriolis Effect, then it must also cause a prevailing drift to the west. It must be both or neither.

In reality, not only do we find that weather systems generally prevail to the east, but also jet streams in both the northern and southern hemisphere, move easterly and at what would be a much greater velocity than the supposed rotation of the earth. There is no reasonable explanation for this on an easterly spinning earth.

A Seattle weather man is asked: Why does weather move from west to east?

> You might think since the Earth rotates toward the east, that our weather would come from the east as we "run into" it. But no, our atmosphere is spinning along with us at nearly the same speed near the ground.

> Instead, weather moves west-to-east thanks to the jet stream, which is a high-altitude wind that moves west-to-east and generally steers our weather.

> It is caused from the temperature difference between our warm equator and cold poles. High pressure at the warm tropics wants to flow toward the low pressure at the cold poles, but the Earth's spin deflects these winds to the east so that they make a circle around the globe (in both hemispheres) moving west to east at mid-latitudes.

> The jet will dip to the north and south as individual low and high pressure systems form, but always carries our weather east.
> (http://www.komonews.com/weather/faq/4347596.html).

A similar question is asked of Aerospaceweb.org. The answer entitled Wind and Earth Rotation gives the common and we think contradictory explanation of how weather systems and jet streams move to the east on a supposed eastward spinning earth. What makes this answer remarkable is its attempt to downplay (!) the effect that earth's rotation has on weather patterns. Despite the detail given, there is more than a hint here that weather patterns do not fit with an eastward spinning earth.

First the question:

> You say that wind, not the Earth's rotation, causes the differences in flight times to the east or west. But what causes the headwind and tailwind? Maybe high up, away from the Earth, the rotation of the atmosphere is lagging behind relative to the rotation of the Earth. You call it a wind, because it is movement of the air relative to the Earth's rotation. So maybe, the difference in travel time is still explained by the rotation of the Earth?

And now the answer:

> You must be referring to several past questions we've answered on differences in flight times between Los Angeles and Bombay, London and New York, and California and Hawaii. In all of those discussions, we explained why flying to the west takes longer than flying to the east and how it is the effect of the wind, and not the rotation of the Earth, that causes these differences.
>
> Now your theory might have some merit if not for one simple fact. If what you say is true, then the wind should blow in the opposite direction of the Earth's rotation since the wind is "lagging behind." But in reality, the Earth rotates to the east and the winds over most of the planet blow to the east as well. These winds are called the Prevailing Westerlies since they blow out of the west and to the east. Furthermore, the Earth rotates fastest at the Equator, so according to your theory, this region is where the winds should blow the hardest. But as you can see below, the region along the Equator is referred to as the Doldrums because there is essentially no prevailing wind in this area.

In the following illustration winds are shown to move in different directions, yet the weather systems themselves prevail to the east. As stated above:

> But in reality, the Earth rotates to the east and the winds over most of the planet blow to the east as well.

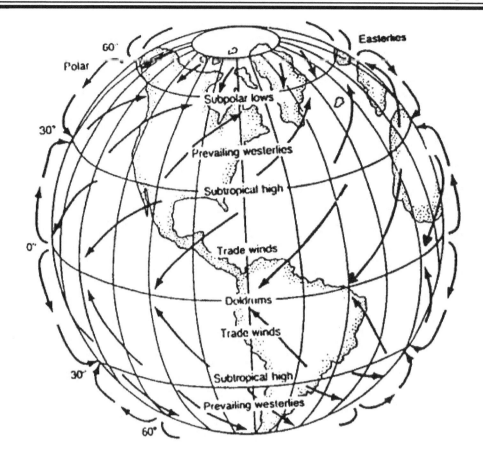

Prevailing Winds

So what does cause the wind to blow in a given direction? While the Earth's rotation does play a role, it is a somewhat indirect one. The primary factor that affects the formation of winds is differences in atmospheric pressure…The principal causes of these differences in pressure are related to the absorption of heat due to solar radiation….

The answer then goes on to explain high and low pressures systems and the effect of sea temperatures upon weather and wind. To conclude there is a word about the Coriolis force:

Nevertheless, you are correct in that the Earth's rotation does play some role in the formation of winds, and therefore has an indirect effect on the difference in east-to-west flight times. The rotation of the Earth creates what is known as the Coriolis force. We've already discussed why air moves from regions of high pressure to those of low pressure. If the Earth did not rotate, wind would blow in a straight line. But since the Earth is rotating beneath the wind, the path it follows becomes a curve. In the Northern Hemisphere, the Earth rotates counter clockwise so the wind is deflected to the right. The Southern Hemisphere rotates clockwise deflecting the wind to the left. Regardless, the Coriolis effect only influences the direction of the wind, not its speed.

So you can see that wind cannot be explained by something as simplistic as the rotation of the Earth…
(Joe Yoon, http://www.aerospaceweb.org/question/atmosphere/q0117.shtml).

To insist upon the rotation of the earth, and yet downplay its effect on the atmosphere is remarkable. Note again:

It is the effect of the wind, and not the rotation of the Earth, that causes these differences. While the Earth's rotation does play a role, it is a somewhat indirect one. The primary factor that affects the formation of winds is differences in atmospheric pressure.

The Earth's rotation does play some role in the formation of winds. So you can see that wind cannot be explained by something as simplistic as the rotation of the Earth.

The questioner believes that something as direct and powerful as the earth's 1038 mph eastward rotation should result in a westward drift of the atmosphere. Why? Common Sense! The answer on the other hand downplays the effect of earth's rotation on the atmosphere. Why? It is clearly difficult to show earth's rotation having a major effect on earth's atmosphere!

This is viewed as a tacit admission that earth's eastward spin is contradictory to earth's eastward weather systems. It is a 180 degree contradiction! Weather patterns should prevail to the west.

It is also worth noting that not only should earth's eastward spin result in the atmosphere moving to the west, but expanding warm air from the sun rising in the east (from the "east spinning earth turning to the rays of the sun") should "push" the atmosphere to the west.

Despite attempts at explanation, the fact remains that there is no valid reason why the atmosphere on an east spinning earth should not move strongly to the west.

Why Do Jet Streams Move to the East?

On a supposed easterly spinning earth we expect to see weather systems prevailing to the west; what we get is the opposite – they prevail to the east. But now further, we also have narrow bands of supercharged wind moving strongly to the east, and, in both hemispheres.

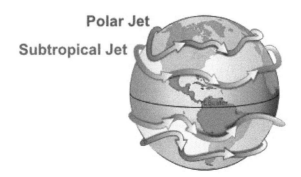

Eastward Jet Streams over an Eastward Spinning Earth!

This picture asks us to believe that jet streams, in both hemispheres, will speed easterly, and at a greater velocity than the easterly spinning earth. This would be in accord with reality if the earth was stationary, but with the factoring in of an eastward spinning earth, it is highly implausible.

The jet stream is a remarkable phenomenon:

> Jet streams are fast flowing, narrow air currents. The main jet streams are located near the tropopause, the transition between the troposphere (where temperature decreases with altitude) and the stratosphere (where temperature increases with altitude). The major jet streams are westerly winds (flowing west to east). Their paths typically have a meandering shape; they may start, stop, split into two or more parts, combine into one stream, or flow in various directions including the opposite direction of most of the jet. The strongest jet streams are the polar jets, at around 7–12 km (23,000–39,000 ft.) above sea level, and the higher and somewhat weaker subtropical jets at around 10–16 km (33,000–52,000 ft.). The Northern Hemisphere and the Southern Hemisphere each have both a polar jet and a subtropical jet. The northern hemisphere polar jet flows over the middle to northern latitudes of North America, Europe, and Asia and their intervening oceans, while the southern hemisphere polar jet mostly circles Antarctica all year round.
>
> Jet streams are caused by a combination of Earth's rotation and atmospheric heating by solar radiation. They form near boundaries of adjacent air masses with significant differences in temperature, such as the polar region and the warmer air towards the equator. (http://en.wikipedia.org/wiki/Jet_stream).

As with so many things in Creation, the explanation of what takes place may not be so difficult, but to explain why or how it takes place may be nearly impossible (especially when denying or ignoring God's workings!). The following is an example:

> I tried to find out what causes the jet stream (the narrow band of high velocity wind in the stratosphere). These flow from west to east at around two hundred miles per hour and meander along in two or three different latitudes. They are only a few kilometers wide. If you get your jet in here, you can shave lots of time off your eastbound trip. Those going westbound are out of luck. I found in my researches that there was no clear explanation ... (http://www.ebtx.com/theory/jetstrem.htm).

The explanation becomes especially difficult when grappling with the jet stream's eastward velocity over an eastward spinning earth. Earth's rotation may be mentioned, but little is said about these "two eastwards."

The question of easterly jet streams was put to the weather team at USA Today. What needs to be noticed in both the Question and the Answer is the little or no reference made to earth's rotation.

> Q: Why do the jet streams travel from west to east in both hemispheres? If the three-cell model of the general circulation of the atmosphere is correct, wouldn't it predict that wind at altitude would travel in an east to west direction at mid-latitudes.

A: First, for those who don't know, the "three cell" model refers to the very general, global pattern of winds. It includes:

- Hadley cells in the tropics <u>with air rising near the equator, sinking at around 30 degrees north and south</u>, and flowing back along the surface toward the equator. [on a equator travelling 1038 mph!].
- Ferrel cells in the middle latitudes with some air flowing along the surface from around 30 degrees toward the poles.
- Polar cells with air on the surface flowing toward the equator to around 60 degrees north or south, where it rises.

This model does a pretty good job of explaining the general flow of winds at the Earth's surface. Air flowing toward the equator in the Hadley cells is turned to the right, or from the east, by the Coriolis force in the Northern Hemisphere and to the left, also from the east, south of the equator. This creates the easterly trade winds. The model also nicely explains westerly surface winds in the middle latitudes of both hemispheres and polar easterlies in the Arctic and Antarctic.

But, as you point out, there is something wrong with the idea of the upper air flow in the middle-latitude Ferrel cell moving toward the equator, which is what the model shows. Winds heading for the equator in both hemispheres are turned toward the west by the Coriolis force. Yet, we know that winds above the middle latitudes would have to be blowing from the equator toward the poles to create the jet streams blowing from the west.

Your question is a good one; the kind that led to a discussion among those on the USA TODAY Weather Team. We agree that the best answer is that the three-cell model is too simple to capture what's really going on in the middle latitudes. As you probably know, the main thing going in the middle latitudes to mess up the simple picture of the three-cell model is the extratropical storms that keep the atmosphere stirred up. These storms carry air both north and south. You could think of the southward flow of upper air shown in the model as representing the average of this flow and also flow by jet streams when they head south, not as an actual picture of all that's going on.

The jet streams blowing from the west begin with higher pressure aloft, say at 30,000 feet, above areas of warm air. The pressure difference begins pushing winds toward the area aloft above cold air. Generally, the warm air is on the equator side and the cold air on the pole side. As the air moves toward the pole the Coriolis force turns it to the right in the Northern Hemisphere and to the left in the Southern Hemisphere. In both cases, this creates jet streams flowing generally from west to east. Jet streams are like the caps, or tops, of boundaries between warm and cold air.
(http://usatoday30.usatoday.com/weather/resources/askjack/waskjet.htm).

This belaboured explanation falls short in explaining the jet stream's eastward velocity, in both hemispheres, and over an eastward spinning earth. As with earth's weather systems prevailing to the east, eastward jet streams are clearly at variance with the idea of an eastward spinning earth.

How Can the Equatorial "Doldrums" Be Spinning At 1038 mph?

It is where the atmosphere is supposed to moving the fastest that we have the doldrums! Could there be a greater contradiction between theory and reality?

Daily hurricanes would be the likely result if the earth is spinning 1038 mph on the Equator! Due to angular momentum extreme weather would be the only result as winds move north and south from the rapidly moving equator to "slower" latitudes. But the reality is quite different; it is at the equator that we have the doldrums!

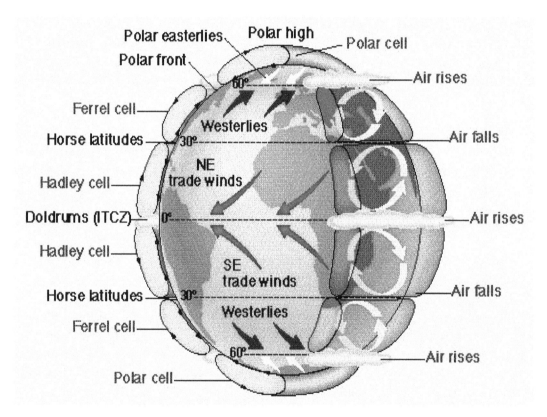

The Equatorial Doldrums and Earth's Weather System

Here rather than continual violent weather sweeping off the equator, we have extended periods of windless calm that would frequently trap sailing ships. Here the air rises nearly vertically (resulting in the calms), not sweeping horizontally to the west as we would expect on an eastward spinning earth. Here, we have an equatorial band of low pressure around the earth, the trade winds from the north and south converge to the doldrums, not vice versa. Here, there can be sudden squalls, but generally it is as the name implies, the doldrums.

All of this is contradictory to the atmosphere at the equator riding on an earth spinning eastward at 1038 mph. You will be pressed to find an explanation for the doldrums that says much about earth's rotation. At 1038 mph there should be a great deal to say.

Why Do Westward Flights Not Arrive Sooner?

Let's replace the atmosphere with aircraft. A supposed spinning earth does not have the effect we would expect it to have on the atmosphere, and now we find it to be the same with air travel. An eastward spinning earth should cause a pronounced westward drift of the atmosphere, and this same eastward spin should result in westward flights arriving sooner. It doesn't happen that way! In both cases it appears that the earth is stationary. The earth does not rush to meet westbound flights.

We saw in the introduction that an object or person can only share fully in the velocity of the earth's rotation if it is directly attached to the earth. This proposition is so obvious it hardly needs to be stated. Once there is a "disconnect" and the object is suspended above the earth, its own velocity, inertia and momentum received from the earth can only decrease. Gravity and the atmosphere may slow the rate of decrease, but the decrease will increasingly become apparent.

An aircraft remaining in the air, flying ever higher, and flying repeatedly from east to west and west to east between two cities on the Equator, must increasingly see its west flight (against earth's eastward rotation) take less time than its easterly flight. Continuing this to an extreme altitude "to just above the atmosphere" the pilot should begin to see the earth rotate beneath the aircraft.

Finally (assuming he has flown high enough), as the atmosphere is said to spin with the earth, if our pilot dives straight down to the Equator, he will experience an overwhelming rush of 1000 mph wind blowing in an easterly direction, as well as having to cope with a 1000 mph ground speed. In reality, this does not happen!

In support of their spinning earth, one would expect a ready answer to this "anomaly." A search of the web will show that while the questions are often clearly stated, the answers are not. Much is made the head or tail winds. Much less is said about earth's rotation. And, virtually nothing is said about the "disconnect" between the aircraft and the earth's rotational speed.

As much is made of head or tail winds on east-west or west-east flights, it need to be pointed out that if the jet stream is ignored, in reality the wind question does not make much difference whether you are flying east or west. What should make a difference is that as the plane "disconnects" from earth, and increasingly loses earth's rotational velocity (It will not take long!), the westbound destination should be rushing to meet the plane. Passengers on the eastbound flight, however, must be prepared for a long haul. It is questionable if the plane will retain enough rotational velocity to even keep up with the earth's rotation, let alone arrive at its destination.

Notice the following response from aerospaceweb to this issue is clearly flawed, and rules out earth's rotation as having any effect on east-west flight times? Though the questioner is in error as to which way the earth is supposed to be rotating, the principle of his question is reasonable.

> QUESTION: When we fly west over the Pacific Ocean (e.g. California to Bombay) it takes about 22 hours to reach the destination, but it only takes 17 hours back. Is this because when flying from California to India the direction of flight is the same as the direction of

the Earth's rotation around its axis, so it takes longer because the destination is moving further away from the plane and the plane is trying to catch the destination? And when flying back the flight direction is opposite of the Earth's rotation and both the airplane and the destination are coming towards each other? Of course the head winds and the tail winds do play quite some role, but I'm guessing that the major factor is the Earth's rotation with respect to the flight direction. Is that correct? -Raj

ANSWER: Speed can be a confusing topic when considered from an aerospace engineering standpoint. For this question, we need to consider two "concepts" of speed. The first is the speed of an object through space, which we will consider as the speed of the Earth's rotation about its axis. If we consider this concept, then you, sitting at your computer, are probably traveling somewhere around 735 mph through space, depending on your location relative to the equator.

The second concept of speed is an object's speed relative to the Earth's surface. In this case, you, sitting at your computer, are traveling at 0 mph relative to the Earth. Now let us consider what would happen if you suddenly stood up and started running. No matter which direction you run, your speed relative to the Earth would be 10 mph. If you were running to the west, against the Earth's rotation, then your speed through space would be 725 mph. Of course, if you ran the opposite way, it would be 745 mph. Your speed relative to the Earth is the same no matter which way you run. It isn't affected by the rotation of the Earth.

Now stop running. If you were to jump straight up in the air, would the Earth rotate beneath you? No, because when you left the Earth's surface, you were traveling at the same speed as the surface, so, in essence, the Earth matched your speed through space while you were in the air! The same condition holds true for an airplane as it travels from Los Angeles to Bombay [Totally false! How can a one second disconnect with earth's rotational speed be compared with a 22 hour disconnect?]. If we were to ignore the winds, no matter which direction you flew from Los Angeles, the speed of the aircraft relative to the Earth would be the same. While the aircraft's speed through space would change, the effect of the Earth's rotation remains constant, and in effect is "cancelled out" no matter which direction you travel. In other words, the speed of the rotation of the Earth is already imparted to the aircraft, and the Earth matches that speed during the entire flight [No! The rotational speed is only imparted up to take off, once aloft the retained rotational speed can only decrease].

So, the end result of that long discussion is that the rotation of the Earth has no effect on the travel time of an aircraft. Actually, as you suggested, it is the headwinds and tailwinds that cause the change in travel times. Sometimes it is hard to believe that the winds can have that much effect, so let us consider the problem a bit more in depth. In the example given, the flight from Bombay to California (east) is 23% shorter than the trip from California to Bombay (west). This means that the speed of the trip east must be 23% faster. The prevailing winds pretty much anywhere that we are talking about blow from west to east, so when we are traveling east, we get a speed gain, and when we travel west, we get a speed penalty. Now, if we are to assume that the winds are identical on both days we fly, then the wind speed only needs to be equal to 11.5% of the aircraft's speed! This would cause a difference between the speed to the west and speed to the east of 23%! The cruise speed of the extended range Boeing 777 is about 550 mph at 35,000 ft. This means that the winds only need a speed of about 65 mph. Believe it or not, 65 mph is a very typical wind speed at such a high altitude…If we wanted to make things more complicated, we could consider a region of high speed flow called the jet stream that flows eastward, and if an aircraft can take advantage of these winds, then the travel time can be reduced further.

So what is the bottom line? The rotation of the Earth does not effect the travel time of an aircraft, and, more importantly, a mere 65 mph wind is more than enough to cause a difference in travel time of five hours when you are traveling long distances! - Doug Jackson, 20 May 2001
(http://www.aerospaceweb.org/question/dynamics/q0027.shtml).

According to this answer, wind blowing at 65 mph has all the effect on flight times, while the supposed rotation of the earth at 1038 mph has none! And further, we are asked to believe that an object disconnected from the earth will retain earth's rotational velocity, whether it is a one-second- jump or a 22 hour flight from Los Angeles to Bombay.

Let's listen to this answer again from aerospaceweb to make certain we heard it right:

If you were to jump straight up in the air, would the Earth rotate beneath you? No, because when you left the Earth's surface, you were traveling at the same speed as the surface, so, in essence, the Earth matched your speed through space while you were in the air! The same condition holds true for an airplane as it travels from Los Angeles to Bombay…In other words, the speed of the rotation of the Earth is already imparted to the aircraft, and the Earth matches that speed during the entire flight.

This cannot possibly be right. Here aerospaceweb is arguing for the retention of motion much in the same of a man walking up and down the aisle of a moving train. It matters not which way he walks, for the full velocity of the train is imparted to him, because he is directly attached to the train. The same is not true of the aircraft or the atmosphere. Which brings back to the title of this section:

THE ATMOSPHERE: IMPOSSIBLE ON A SPEEDING EARTH

Part V: Further Evidence

Einstein and "Shrinking Interferometer Arms" to the Rescue

A study of the above will show that heliocentricity is not the open and shut case that is assumed. The famous and oft-repeated Michelson-Morley experiment was a wakeup call that this is in fact the case! In this experiment two simultaneous light beams are sent out and back at right angles along two arms of an interferometer. One is sent and returns in the direction of the earth's assumed movement around the sun, the other is flashed over the same distance, but at right angles. The beam sent at right angles should return slightly sooner. This is because the amount of time the other beam spends moving with the orbital velocity of the earth (66,780 mph) and through the medium of space (whatever medium it may contain) is not enough to compensate for the time it spends returning against this velocity. Though oft repeated, and unto our present day with ever greater sophistication, the results are the same, the light beams return at about the same time. Based on this experiment, the earth shows little or no movement around the sun!

When first performed the Michelson-Morley experiment caused a convulsion in the scientific community. An optical experiment has denied the motion of the earth! "Why, when the earth is moving does it appear to stand still?" The "anomaly" could no longer be tolerated. It was only with Albert Einstein and his special theory of relativity in 1905 that an "answer was found".

Primary to Einstein's theory was the incorporation of the bizarre Fitzgerald Contraction that was formulated as an immediate response to Michelson-Morley. Fitzgerald conveniently theorized that an object would contract in the direction of its high velocity (that is, it would get thinner!). The bearing this would have for the arms of Michelson and Morley's interferometer is obvious. The reason why the right angle light beam had not returned sooner than the beam parallel to earth's supposed movement is because the arm conveying the parallel beam had shrunk!

We will indeed weave our little webs! Few today realize that the primary purpose of Einstein's 1905 Special Relativity Theory was to give a response to the failure of Michelson-Morley and other light experiments to demonstrate earth-motion. For a full account of the relation of Einstein's special and general theories of relativity to geocentricity see Malcolm Bowden, True Science Agrees with the Bible; and Geocentricity by Gerardus Bouw.

Three Aspects of Geocentricity

The following is a list of the various factors and experiments that relate to three basic areas of Geocentricity.

Earth's "Rotation"

Coriolis effect
Earth's bulge
Foucault pendulum

Sagnac experiment
Michelson Gale experiment
Stationary satellite
Violating the speed of light
Mach's Principle,
Barbour and Bertotti

Earth's "Movement Around the Sun"

Aberration
Star streaming
Parallax
Doppler effect
Fresnell drag
Airy's failure
Michelson-Morley experiment(s)
Dayton Miller's experiments
Polarization experiments
Mutual inductance experiment
Trouton-Noble experiment
Stephan Marinov's experiments

Earth at the Center of the Universe

Varshni's quasar redshifts
Barr effect
Galactic shells
Microwave background

See Gerardus Bouw, among others, for an examination of each of these in his book, Geocentricity.

Experiments That Failed to Show the Earth in Motion

The following is from Malcolm Bowden – a leading Creation Scientist in the UK. Since the publication of his important book True Science Agrees with the Bible (1998) he has argued strongly in favour of geocentricity.

> Geocentrists are ridiculed as "unscientific" and "getting their science from the Bible". However, there are four experiments which clearly point to a geocentric universe. Only the Michelson-Morley is ever referred to; the other three are never mentioned in any university anywhere in the world.

(a) The Michelson-Morley experiment

Most scientists know about the Michelson-Morely experiment. It was carried out to check that the velocity of the earth round the sun was about 30km/sec as it moved through the aether. When it found hardly any movement at all, the result stunned the scientific community! Little of this reached the ears of the public and this result had to be "explained away".

There is a simple model that can be pictured to explain the reason for the experiment. Imagine that you are on a lake in a small boat with a very quiet engine (the earth), and not far away is a huge liner (the sun). You are at the centre of the lake and the shore is a long way off but you can see mountains on it etc. You notice that the shore (the stars) is going past the large ship fairly quickly, and you realise that either (i) you are circling the large ship OR (ii) the large ship is circling you - and you cannot immediately tell which one is circling which. You know the distance between the two ships and timing how long it takes for the shore to make a complete circle (1 year), you can say that either the large ship is going round you at 30mph or you are going round it at that speed.

There is a very simple test that will tell you which one is circling which. What can you do to find out??? The answer is very simple. You put your hand in the water (the ether)!!! If you are moving through the water, then it is you going round the large ship, and you can check your speed through the water to see if it is 30 mph. If it is, then the large ship must be stationary. HOWEVER, if you find that you are stationary in the water, then it must be the large ship that is GOING ROUND YOU.

The MM experiment showed that the earth was (almost) stationary! So they had to invent the Fitzgerald-Lorentz contraction, and eventually Einstein swept the whole problem under the carpet by mathematically removing the aether (the water). That this brought huge problems into scientific theories was ignored, and false evidence was produced (Eclipse, travelling clocks, perihelion precession of Mercury) to support the theory. There have been many attacks upon the theory, but so powerful are the forces that support it that they have had little publicity or real damaging effect upon the "scientific" acceptance of the theory even today.

It is the following three experiments that are never taught to science undergraduates.

(b) The Michelson-Gale Experiment.

(Reference - Astrophysical Journal 1925 v 61 pp 140-5). This detected the aether passing the surface of the earth with an accuracy of 2% of the speed of the daily rotation of the earth! Thus, the Michelson-Morely experiment detected no movement of the earth around the sun, yet the Michelson-Gale experiment measured the earth's rotation (or the aether's rotation around the earth!) to within 2%! This surely speaks volumes for geocentricity. [This therefore proved the existence of the aether, which Einstein sought to deny in his answer to the Michelson-Morley experiment].

(c) Airy's Failure

(Reference - Proc. Roy. Soc. London v 20 p 35). Telescopes [would] have to be very slightly tilted to get the starlight going down the axis of the tube because of the earth's "speed around the sun". Airey filled a telescope with water that greatly slowed down the speed of the light inside the telescope and found that he did not have to change the angle of the telescope. This showed that **the starlight was already coming in at the original measured angle so that no change was needed**. This demonstrated that it was the stars moving relative to a stationary earth and not the fast orbiting earth moving relative to the comparatively stationary stars. If it was the telescope moving he would have had to change the angle.

(Imagine the telescope like a tube, sloped so that the light from one star hits the bottom of the tube. Even if the starlight is slowed down inside the tube (using water), it will still hit the bottom of the tube because its direction is already determined. If it were the tube that was moving, slowing down the starlight would mean that the angle of the tube would have to change for the light to hit the bottom of the tube).

It is interesting that the original short two page report merely lists the results and discusses the accuracy of the telescope used. There is not the slightest reference to the astonishing result that this experiment demonstrates - that the stars are moving round the stationary earth. [Sir George Biddell Airy, Astronomer Royal from 1835 to 1881, established Greenwich as the location of the prime meridian].

(d) The Sagnac Experiment

(Reference - Comptes Rendus 1913 v157 p 708-710 and 1410-3) Sagnac rotated a table at 2 revs/sec complete with light and mirrors and camera with the light being passed in opposite directions around the table between the mirrors. The rotation of the whole apparatus was detected by the movement of the interference fringes on the target where they were recombined. This proved that there IS an aether that the light has to pass through and this completely destroys Einstein's theory of Relativity that says there is no aether. It is for this reason that this experiment is completely ignored by scientists. More recently Kantor has found the same result with similar apparatus.

To summarise:

(A) The Sagnac experiment proved that there WAS an aether which could be used as a reference frame for movements. This demolished Einstein's theories of Relativity.

(B) Using the ether as a frame of reference, the Michelson-Morley experiment showed that we were NOT going round the sun.

(C) Airey's experiment proved that the starlight was already coming into the earth at an angle, being carried along by the rotating aether.

(D) The Michelson-Gale experiment showed that the aether was going round the stationary earth 1 rotation per day. (The alternative that the earth was spinning 1 rotation per day inside a stationary aether is disproven by Airey's experiment. Note - to be pedantic, Airey's experiment involved measurements of a small angle due to the high 30Km/s "speed of the earth around the sun". The rotation of the earth at the equator is only .45Km/s and is too slow to register any angle change.)

These last three experiments are never taught at universities, so consequently, scientists, including most Christian creationists, are ignorant of this evidence for geocentricity. I asked three Christian physicists if they had ever heard of them; not one had! In October 2004 I commented on the UK creation forum - "Re decrease in the speed of light - It MIGHT be constant now, but most certainly was not in the past; it was still falling until the 1950's. In addition, Sagnac's experiment proved that there IS an aether, whilst Einstein's Relativity Theorem is based on it NOT existing. Could I ask if ANYONE who did science at any university if they were ever told about Sagnac's simple experiment? I rather doubt it. So the fables of Relativity are passed down from generation to generation. What happened to truth?

I have just (1 March 2005) received an interesting response - "My agreement with all below [i.e. my comment "above"]. After 35 years as a professional physicist, with a thesis in relativity, I only learned of Sagnac's experiment last year...... R."

In January 2007 another correspondent complained that his professors never mentioned these important experiments -

"Dear Mr. Bowden, Thank you for your enjoyable and well-written website. I've enjoyed visiting there today. I was especially interested in your comments on geocentricity, which (as noted) are controversial. The amazing thing is that NONE of the experiments cited were ever discussed in my undergraduate education, nor the implications cited...."

"...All my life, I have heard the story of how Copernicus' theory came to prevail. I would have thought that major experimental evidence already in existence and calling the theory into question would have at least been cited; and given the importance of some of the philosophical extrapolations on cosmology, theology, space exploration and public education in the United States, one would have also thought that the matter would have been intensely investigated until a resolution of the data with the theory could be obtained. One feels cheated as a student, of course, to keep finding twenty-five years later these bodies of contrarian evidence that never are mentioned in the classroom, unless a student has already researched the topics and brings them up..." (Emphasis MB).

Is it any wonder, therefore, that Christian geocentrists find their most vociferous opponents are fellow Christian creationists to whom geocentricity comes as a shock. They do not want to be tarred with such a heretical brush that will only increase the great ridicule they are

already receiving for their stance against evolution?
(http://www.mbowden.surf3.net/Geocexpl.htm)

Two Common Arguments Against Geocentricity

The speed with which the stars must travel around the stationary earth, and the space program, are generally the two biggest arguments against Geocentric position. Malcolm Bowden comments:

The Rapid Rotation of the Universe

How can the universe rotate so rapidly without disintegrating? There is growing evidence that the ether has "Planck density" - it is extremely dense and the sun and planets are like corks in very dense water comparatively. This whole universe sweeps round the earth because otherwise it would collapse in on itself due to its density. The mechanics of this system forces the other planets etc. to describe ellipses in their orbit around the sun.

Ernst Mach proposed that it is the weight of the stars circling the earth that drags Foucault pendulums around, creates Coriolis forces in the air that give the cyclones to our weather etc. Barbour and Bertotti (Il Nuovo Cimento 32B(1):1-27, 11 March 1977) proved that a hollow sphere (the universe) rotating around a solid sphere inside (the earth) produced exactly the same results of Coriolis forces, dragging of Foucault pendulums etc. that are put forward as "proofs" of heliocentricity! This paper gives several other confirmations of the superiority of the geocentric model.

Thus, there is evidence that the earth is NOT moving around the sun, but either the aether is moving around the earth carrying the planets with it, or the earth is spinning on its axis. The most likely model is that the aether is rotating around the earth as calculations show that if it did not, it would rapidly collapse upon itself.

The Space Program

Some may question if the geocentric model would make it impossible for NASA to predict spacecraft orbits etc. This is easily dealt with.

Assume you are looking at an orrery - a mechanical machine with the planets on long arms rotating around the sun which is at the centre. In this machine the sun is stationary at the centre and the planets rotate around it and also spin on their axis. This is the accepted way in which the planets move around the sun. Now imagine that, while it is working, you pick the whole machine up by holding the earth. Everything now rotates about the earth, but their relative positions as they go round the sun and to each other are exactly the same as before. Einstein's relativity does not come into it.

What people do not realise is that NASA works out every spacecraft trajectory related to the earth - as though the earth were the centre of the planetary system. This is NOT presented as further scientific evidence as it is only used to make the maths easier, but it is interesting nevertheless. (Ibid.).

Malcolm Bowden has presented a number of helpful video's on Geocentricity. Two recent ones include:

Geocentricity: Second Version
http://www.youtube.com/watch?v=CUdaTH3T3Ok

Geocentricity Explains the Seasons http://www.youtube.com/watch?v=CUdaTH3T3Ok

The Question of Equivalence

Gerardus Bouw and other geocentrists believe that the universe is so designed that absolute scientific proof for either view is not possible. One would have to be outside the universe looking in, to determine for certain the question of relative motion. Phenomena such as the Coriolis effect and the Foucault pendulum would be the same whether the earth is spinning or the universe is revolving around the earth. As the renowned astronomer Sir Fred Hoyle said:

> We know that the difference between a heliocentric theory and a geocentric theory is one of relative motion only, and that such a difference has no physical significance. (*Astronomy and Cosmology – A Modern Course*, p.416).

Nevertheless, if one view is right and the other wrong, how could the resulting phenomena of each be entirely equivalent?

Conclusion

In this inquiry, it is the first concern of the Bible believer to seek out what Scripture itself says about this most fundamental aspect of God's creation. It is at this point that many of the creationist rebuttals of geocentricity are flawed. A search of the net will show that they have spent little time with very few of the considerable number of Scripture passages listed above.

Finally, Ponder a Scripture like I Corinthians 1:19:

> *For it is written, I will destroy the wisdom of the wise, and will bring to nothing the understanding of the prudent.*

Of all of the subjects involving man's self-proclaimed wisdom, it would be difficult to imagine a greater shock than to be found to be wrong on this one. The lead article in the 10 June 2006 issue of New Scientist may be a pointer of thing things to come. Under the caption WANT TO MAKE SENSE OF THE UNIVERSE? LET IT SPIN, Marcus Chown writes:

> Look up at the sky. Almost everything out there is spinning around: stars, galaxies, planets, moons - they are all rotating. Yet physicists believe that the universe itself is not revolving. Why?

> It's a question that Pawel Mazur can't answer. Mazur, a physicist at the University of South Carolina in Columbia, is one of a number who think it is entirely possible that our universe is spinning on an axis. If these people are right, it could make understanding the universe a whole lot simpler.

In a letter to the same magazine the following week, an exasperated reader thinks that we now need a "blank sheet of paper and start over" approach to the physics and cosmology of the universe. But for us, the stars in their courses and the earth at rest (stable that it cannot be moved, I Chr. 16:30) seems clearly to be the Scripture cosmology.

And, with this we are at rest

Postscript:

Among others, reference should be made to the important work of Dr. Yasser Ragab Shaban. He was born in Poland and raised in Egypt. Along with considerable and exceptional qualifications, he received a Bachelor of Nuclear Engineering from the University of Alexandria; and a Master of Science in Nuclear Engineering, followed by a Ph. D in Nuclear Engineering from the University of Illinois. His book *The Verses of Deus* (taken from the fact that he believes the Bible teaches geocentricity) is highly technical, but his conclusions can be readily understood.

In my presentation I came to the view that one of the best *nearby* scientific arguments for a fixed earth, is the atmosphere and east—west plane travel. It was good to find that this learned Scientist came to the same conclusion.

the
BIBLE
FOR
TODAY

900 Park Avenue
Collingswood, NJ 08108
Phone: 856-854-4452
www.BibleForToday.org

BFT #4054